AUTHORS

Paolo Crippa (23 April 1978) has been cultivating a passion for Italian history, especially World War II, since high school. His research focuses mainly on the field of military history and in particular on armoured units from the 1930s until the end of World War II. In 2006, he published his first volume, 'I Reparti Corazzati della Repubblica Sociale Italiana 1943/1945', the first organic research completed and published in Italy on the subject, which was followed in the following years by four more books with Marvia Edizioni and five with Mattioli 1885. He has more than fifty articles to his credit for the magazines Milites, Historica Nuova, SGM - Second World War, Batailes & Blindes, Ritterkreuz, Fronti di Guerra, Mezzi Corazzati, Storia & Battaglie, Il Carrista d'Italia, Umago Viva, La Martinella, Storia del Novecento and Uniformi, both as an author and in collaboration with other researchers, and has collaborated and consulted other authors in the drafting of historical-uniformological texts. He has taken part in broadcasts of the on-line television network Legnano Web TV and in broadcasts of Radio RAI - Friuli Venezia Giulia, and has conducted several conferences for the Associazione Nazionale Carristi d'Italia. He carries out information activities on the subject of the foibe and the Giuliano-Dalmatian Exodus, both through his Facebook page and with thematic conferences held in high schools and for the ANVGD (Associazione Nazionale Venezia Giulia e Dalmazia). Since 2019 he has been collaborating with Luca Cristini Editore in the realisation of the series "Witness to War" and since 2020 he is its Director.

Daniele Notaro, born on 22 January 2002 in Lavagna, is a History student at the University of Genoa. Since his early teens he has cultivated a passion for the Second World War, focusing in particular on the events of the Regio Esercito in the 1930s and 1940s. Other topics of interest to him are the cobelligerent armed forces, the events of the Autonomous Units of the Italian Resistance and the Italian coastal defence from the 1930s to the end of the Second World War. He started to publish his first writings on the Tank Encyclopedia site in 2022 and was a contributor to the journal Military History in his last period.

PUBLISHING'S NOTES

None of unpublished images or text of our book may be reproduced in any format without the expressed written permission of Luca Cristini Editore (already Soldiershop.com) when not indicate as marked with license creative commons 3.0 or 4.0. Luca Cristini Editore has made every reasonable effort to locate, contact and acknowledge rights holders and to correctly apply terms and conditions to Content.

Every effort has been made to trace the copyright of all the photographs. If there are unintentional omissions, please contact the publisher in writing at: info@soldiershop.com, who will correct all subsequent editions.

Our trademark: Luca Cristini Editore©, and the names of our series & brand: Soldiershop, Witness to war, Museum book, Bookmoon, Soldiers&Weapons, Battlefield, War in colour, Historical Biographies, Darwin's view, Fabula, Altrastoria, Italia Storica Ebook, Witness To History, Soldiers, Weapons & Uniforms, Storia etc. are herein © by Luca Cristini Editore.

LICENSES COMMONS

This book may utilize part of material marked with license creative commons 3.0 or 4.0 (CC BY 4.0), (CC BY-ND 4.0), (CC BY-SA 4.0) or (CC0 1.0). We give appropriate attribution credit and indicate if change were made in the acknowledgments field. Our WTW books series utilize only fonts licensed under the SIL Open Font License or other free use license.

For a complete list of Soldiershop titles please contact Luca Cristini Editore on our website: www.soldiershop.com or www.cristinieditore.com. E-mail: info@soldiershop.com

Title: ALBA, A DISPUTED CITY 1944-1945 Code.: **WTW-060 EN**
By Paolo Crippa and Daniele Notaro
ISBN code: 9791255891345. First edition June 2024.
Language: English; size: 177,8x254mm Cover & Art Design: Luca S. Cristini

WITNESS TO WAR (SOLDIERSHOP) is a trademark of Luca Cristini Editore, via Orio, 33D - 24050 Zanica (BG) ITALY.

WITNESS TO WAR

ALBA, A DISPUTED CITY 1944-1945

PHOTOS & IMAGES FROM WORLD WARTIME ARCHIVES

PAOLO CRIPPA - DANIELE NOTARO

BOOKS TO COLLECT

CONTENTS

Introduction..5

The battles for Alba..7

    La Repubblica partigiana di Alba...8

    The 'liberation' of Alba..10

        Appendix: Report of 'Captain Fede', commander of the Alba square, on the partisan defence of the city...16

    The battle from April 1945 and the fall of the city.....................................19

        Appendix: the report on the battle of 15 April 1945, written by the commander of the 2nd Battalion Arditi Fanti of the R.A.P...................................23

The situation of the partisan forces in the Langhe from summer 1944 to May 1945.....45

    Autonomous Departments..45

    Garibaldi Departments..51

    G.L. Departments...52

    Matteotti Departments..53

R.S.I. units garrisoned in Alba from Summer 1944 to May 1945..................71

    II Battalion Arditi Fanti...72

    III Alpine Armed Forces Battalion...78

    X Special Artillery Group...79

    Autonomous Cavalry Department...82

    1st Light Tank Company...83

Bibliography..96

INTRODUCTION

The city of Alba is an important town in the Langhe in the province of Cuneo, which became famous in the post-war period mainly thanks to the writings of Beppe Fenoglio, who fictionalised many of his personal events, which he experienced while he was a partisan in the area.
In fact, the town of Alba was the backdrop to the clashes between partisans and Axis troops between 1944 and 1945 and was even occupied by Resistance forces in October 1944, who, however, retained control for only a few days, the famous '23 days of Alba', described by Beppe Fenoglio in his book of the same name.
The city was again attacked by partisans on 15 April 1945, in a clash that lasted all day, but did not dislodge the Republican garrison from the city, and it was not until 26 April that the partisans of the II 'Langhe' Division and the 21st Matteotti 'Fratelli Ambrogio' Brigade finally entered the city, with the surrender of the Italian Social Republic forces.
This publication examines the events that took place in the Langhe city between 1944 and 1945, with descriptions of the partisan and republican units that clashed in the Langhe. Reproductions of a good number of original documents from both factions complete the text.

Acknowledgements

This volume is dedicated to the memory of Alfredo Giaroni, who passed away prematurely. We sincerely thank his wife Ersilia Gianlorenzi, for kindly consenting to the publication of unpublished photographs of her father-in-law Carlo, who was a very young Cavalryman in the Autonomous Cavalry Department of the R.A.P. in Alba.
In writing this book, we would like to remember other people who contributed by providing images, documentation, bibliography and information. In particular, we would like to thank for their help, in strict alphabetical order, Mattia Barbero, Carlo Cucut (who, in addition to copious documentation, also provided numerous images from Attilio Viziano's archive), Marcello Gallesi, who has unfortunately left us, Luigi Manes, Pierfranco Malfettani and Tommaso Murino.

▲Left: Ardito badge, in the version made during the R.S.I., which had the word 'Italia' on the gladius guard instead of the Savoy motto 'FERT'. From 20 December 1944, it was awarded to soldiers employed in counter-band combat who had participated in at least three field operations. Right: ribbon distributed to R.S.I. soldiers engaged in anti-partisan operations. This picture shows the version with green ribbon (g.c. My Militaria).

▲ A FIAT 626 truck of the Raggruppamento 'Cacciatori degli Appennini' (Apennine Hunters' Regiment) with soldiers of the III G.N.R. Battalion and Auxiliaries on board, photographed at the end of the war during the retreat towards Strambino Romano. In the last months of the war, the unit's vehicles were gradually modified to be fuelled with gasogen, due to the shortage of fuel (Pisanò).

▼ The Partisan Command of the 'Matteotti' formations advances towards Alba, while the Republican garrison leaves the city on 10 October 1944.

THE BATTLES FOR ALBA

Alba had been occupied in September 1943, after the Armistice of 8 September, by German SS units. It was only in the first half of 1944, many months after the formation of the Italian Social Republic, that the Germans were replaced by Italian units in the city's garrison: a detachment of the Autonomous Mobile Legion 'Ettore Muti'.
In the second half of 1944, the Tanaro valley, and the Piedmontese Langhe in general, began to become heavily contested territory by the Social Republic and the partisans, who were gaining a foothold in the region. In particular, the city of Alba, located on the right bank of the Tanaro river, a few kilometres from the entrance to a long valley traced by the river between the large hill groups of the upper Monferrato and the Langhe, represented in the republican strategy the most advanced garrison position towards the areas controlled by the partisans.
On 7 August, the 2nd 'Hunters of the Apennines' Regiment of the Centro Addestramento Reparti Speciali (Special Forces Training Centre), under the command of Colonel Aurelio Languasco[1] also took up positions in the city. The C.A.R.S. units stationed in Piedmont, which constituted the so-called 'Farina Regiment', carried out raids in the Langhe with the 1st Mobile Black Brigade and SS units throughout August. At the end of the month, a strong concentration of partisans in retreat was reported around Monforte d'Alba (CN): the German Command issued an order to carry out a counter-band operation on September 1st, in which the 1st and 2nd "Cacciatori degli Appennini" Regiments, a truck unit of the 1st Mobile Black Brigade, 4 Ukrainian Wehrmacht Companies and a section of 3 47/32 pieces of the Italian SS Heldmann Group took part. The units moved out shortly after 6 a.m., but the Resistance units, which had detected the troop movements, began to move away. Once the surprise effect wore off, the firefights were limited and the results were negligible (the 2nd Hunters Regiment still lost one man).
In the meantime, a strong friction had arisen in Alba between the 'Cacciatori degli Appennini' Regiment and the 'Muti' Legion's unit, which acted almost completely autonomously and wanted to have command of the town garrison. According to the recollections of the bishop of Alba, Monsignor Luigi Grassi, the situation was indeed tense: '[...] *The Muti unit was working on its own and in conflict with the 2nd Hunters because each wanted to hold command of the garrison, trying to trip each other up*'[2]. For this reason, the 'Muti' fell back to other positions at the end of August, leaving the city in the hands of the 'Cacciatori' Regiment.

---

1 The Regiment was formed as follows:
- Command
- I G.N.R. Battalion out of 3 Companies under the command of Major Vallocchia;
- II Battalion G.N.R. out of 3 Companies under the command of Major Rose;
- III Carabinieri Battalion out of 3 Companies under the command of Lieutenant Colonel Dal Piaz.

2 "Personal recollections", article by Monsignor Lugi Grassi from 1946, cited in the bibliography.

The Partisan Republic of Alba

At the end of the summer, the situation in the Langhe worsened for the Italian Social Republic, due to the increased activity of the gangs commanded by 'Mauri', who completely controlled the Alba area, and at the end of September an event occurred that would later deliver the town into Mauri's hands. In fact, the 2nd Regiment of the 'Cacciatori degli Appennini' was recalled to Ceva, the headquarters of the C.A.R.S. by order of General Del Giudice, commander of the Special Forces Training Centre, and the garrison of Alba was entrusted to the 2nd Alpine Battalion 'Cadore' of the 1st Regiment 'Cacciatori degli Appennini', which took up its position on 3 October, under the command of Colonel Ippolito Radaelli. He was a man held in high esteem by the city's bishop ('[...] *a man and a battalion that behaved exemplarily in the few days they stayed with us*'). However, the department's presence in the city was very short-lived.

In the preceding weeks, the town had been subjected to repeated, small but wearisome night attacks by the partisans, especially in the periphery, towards the Republican military checkpoints and the most exposed barracks. The conviction grew in the city's military command that it was probably necessary to abandon the city before it became indefensible. Consequently, on 10 October, the town of Alba was occupied at noon, without a shot being fired, by partisans from the 1st Alpine Divisions Group (Brigades "Belbo", "Canale" and "Alba"), a flying squad from the 7th "Giustizia e Libertà" Band and the "Michel" Detachment[3] of the VI Garibaldi Division, after they had forced the Republican garrison, made up of the "Cadore" Battalion and a garrison of 40 men from the G.N.R., to evacuate the city following the mediation of the bishop, Monsignor Luigi Maria Grassi.

The occupation of the city took place unbeknownst to the commands of the VI Garibaldi Division and the 48th Brigade and the participation of Michel's detachment in the action in the city was a coincidence due to the encounter between this unit - employed in a normal patrol action - and the forces advancing towards Alba.

Giovanni Latilla 'Nanni', commander of the VI Garibaldi Division, stated on 12 October: *The occupation of Alba took place without Mauri or the G.L. being informed of the VI Division and 48 Brigade commanders, as it would have been logical to do in the spirit of close cooperation between all the partisan formations before such an important decision was taken.* [4]

The fascist garrison left Alba in an almost orderly column without leaving their weapons, heading north (according to a partisan source, only a few sporadic mortar rounds were fired at the retreating Republican soldiers). Monsignor Grassi describes the departure of the Republican garrison in his memoirs as follows: '*After 10 days or a little more the battalion already received the order to leave... without any troops being announced to supplement the garrison. Colonel Redaelli was making preparations to leave and on Monday 9 October he came to take leave of me and to tell me his concern for the town, and that having spoken with his superiors, they had come to the idea of handing the town over peacefully to Major Mauri's Badogliani to save it from the dangers presented the day before to the Prefect of Cuneo himself, by the town Commissioner*'.

---
[3] The unit is named after its commander Amilcare Ghibellini 'Michel', a former sergeant major of the Alpine troops born in 1911.
[4] Taken from Toscani, 'Con i partigiani in Valbormida, Valle Uzzone, Velle Belbo - Langhe', cited in bibliography.

It has long been debated whether there was an agreement between the fascist military and the Resistance for a bloodless handover of control of the town, but the situation is certainly much more complex; in fact, it is likely that there was in fact an 'agreement' between the commander of the 'Cadore' Battalion and his military superiors to avoid a bloody clash against the partisans, who at that stage seemed to have the objective of settling in the town, as there were no republican forces available to reinforce the garrison. However, it should be emphasised that the Garibaldi Brigades were also opposed to the occupation of the town, as they considered the step premature '*given the limited possibility of defending Alba in the event of an offensive return of the enemy in force*' and considered it a serious mistake to have allowed the fascists to leave the garrison '*with all their weapons and material, while there was the possibility of taking 300 Alpine soldiers and important armaments prisoner*'. The conquest of Alba, in essence, therefore had for the autonomi a value above all of political and prestige, because the partisan military commanders were aware that they did not have the possibility of holding the city for long. Command of the square was assumed by Carlo Alberto Morelli 'Carletto', commander of the 'Belbo' Brigade of the II Langhe Division, later replaced by Enzo Bramardi 'Captain Fede'.

A Liberation Committee was set up with members chosen from among the leading local politicians to manage the civil administration, thus beginning the epic of the so-called 'Republic of Alba'. The partisans controlled the entire Tanaro embankment to the north, as far as the Pollenzo bridge, which was controlled by the Germans, who were based in the former Savoy residence of the Pollenzo hunting estate.

However, the question arises as to why the partisan commands had not done better to give up their occupation of the city, remaining firmly in their positions in the surrounding hills, given that the incipient bad weather was likely to slow down the partisan offensives in Piedmont and the Allies on the southern front. Mauri himself provides the answer in his memoirs[5] : '*The Allied offensive has come to a halt on the Gothic line, but it will soon be resumed, there is no doubt. Soon the whole of Piedmont, the whole of Italy will be free. Even Temple is so sure of that. But I'm glad you confirm it.*
- *Where will we be at Christmas, Temple?* -
- *In Turin, would you like to bet? I'll pawn a gold chronometer*-'.

Mauri was therefore convinced that the lull in the Allied offensive was only temporary and would soon resume, leading inevitably to the liberation of northern Italy. In Mauri's vision, therefore, the city of Alba necessarily became the capital of an embryonic state within the Italian Social Republic: '*The Langhe has now become a country entirely our own, a small free state within the territory of the Fascist Social Republic. Throughout the area included, in the great arc of the Tanaro river, from Ceva to Asti, the partisan tricolour waves in defiance and along the sonorous waters of the river, in which the blood of the contenders is mixed and dispersed, our units stand guard. The small state comprises more than a hundred villages with a few hundred thousand inhabitants. The municipal administration is governed by freely elected committees, mayors and juntas... Major Peschiera implanted the complex organisation of Civil Affairs to regulate relations with the municipal administrations, regulate requisitions, and collect taxes. The police service is carried out by Lieutenant Marino's Carabinieri stations, which were implanted in the main concentrics. The administration of*

---

5 From 'With Freedom and for Freedom', work cited in the bibliography.

justice, including criminal and civil disputes between locals, is regulated by the divisional courts, under the vigilant control of the Justices. The health service now has the hospitals of Murazzano and Cortemilia at its disposal... The small state is thus not just a simple and empty expression; it is something alive and operating. Only the capital is missing... Let us look at Alba the capital of the Langhe. The little town lying on the banks of the Tanaro draws us in inadvertently, irresistibly[6]. Mauri, however, was initially sceptical about the possibility of being able to maintain a constant garrison over the city, so much so that, for the first two nights following the 'liberation', he ordered his men to fall back to their original positions, so as not to be too exposed to possible dangers. The stable and continuous occupation of the town actually began after the occurrence of certain events that disturbed public order, episodes that required a constant military presence day and night.

Thus, a 'Partisan Republic' was established in Alba, a de facto provisional state entity, removed from the influence of the authorities of the Italian Social Republic and governed by the partisans, according to a republican mode. The command of the square was entrusted to Lieutenant Carlo Alberto Morelli 'Carletto', commander of the 'Belbo' Brigade of the II 'Langhe' Division, later replaced by Enzo Bramardi 'Captain Fede', while a National Liberation Committee was set up to manage the civil administration, made up of members chosen from among the leading local anti-fascist political figures. The civil authorities regulated food requisitions, gave impetus to the machine shops to start producing weapons, had the 'Gazzetta Piemontese', Alba's first free newspaper, printed, ordered distilleries to produce alcohol to replace petrol, given the almost total lack of fuel, and even celebrated a wedding. Outside the city, partisan units controlled the entire Tanaro riverbank to the north, as far as the Pollenzo bridge, where German units were based at the former Savoy hunting estate in Pollenzo. Popular municipal councils were also set up, first elected by a show of hands, and then with ballots counted in the presence of the voters, in the various localities of the area liberated from the presence of the Italo-German troops. The first of these councils was elected in Vinchio on 17 September, and a few days later councils were elected in the Tiglione valley and other liberated areas. A police corps was set up for public order and with political attributions: this had the task of *'providing for the neutralisation and repression... of the disruptive activity that republican, ex-fascist, pro-republican, pro-German fascist elements are carrying out in every municipality of the liberated area, in order to break the single national anti-fascist front'*.

The 'liberation' of Alba

In the days following the occupation of the city, Piedmont's High Commissioner Zerbino and Turin's Federal Commissioner Solaro decided to give the partisan formations a shot in the arm by 'liberating' the Langhe, immediately after the complete reoccupation of Valdossola, which was underway in those days. Towards the end of the month, the Anti-Partisan Regiment was then ordered to converge on Alba, while an ultimatum was sent to the self-styled Partisan Republic with the order to evacuate the city. On 26 October, thanks to the intervention of the bishop, who did not want armed clashes to take place in the town, which would have seriously endangered the population, a meeting was held in

---

6 From 'With Freedom and for Freedom', work cited in the bibliography.

Santa Vittoria d'Alba between the partisan commander 'Mauri' and Duccio Galimberti, leader of 'Giustizia e Libertà', on the one hand, and the High Commissioner for Piedmont, Zerbino, and the Federal Commissioner for Turin, Solaro, on the other. Between 30th and 31st October, three more meetings were held between Major Mauri and High Commissioner Zerbino, again with the mediation of Monsignor Grossi, in Barbaresco, Mussotto and Cinzano; before signing an agreement, Zerbino took his time asking for a fourth meeting, to which Mauri, however, only sent one of his representatives. On their return from this last meeting, the Resistance representatives informed Major Mauri of the Republicans' proposal. The partisan commander summed up the discussion with his representatives in his memoirs as follows: '*If at the first cannon shot I raise the white flag on the cathedral bell tower, they will give me time to retreat. "What should we do?" asked Fede (the commander of the Alba Piazza). "At the first shot of the cannon raise the tricolour on the bell tower"*.

Meanwhile, on 30 October, Colonel Ruta, commander of the Regiment, received the order to attack the town from High Commissioner Zerbino. In fact, we read in the 'Report on the operations carried out on 31 October - 1-2 November 1944 for the liberation of Alba, already occupied by outlaws' by Colonel Ruta to the Army General Staff: '*On 30 October 1944, I received the order from dr. Zerbino, Extraordinary Commissioner for Piedmont, in the presence of the Federal Commissioner of the P. F. R. and the Chief of the Province of Cuneo, to concretise the order of operations for the liberation of Alba, which had passed under the control of the rebels, and to assume command of the troops necessary to carry out the action. Taking into account the task and the particular enemy situation, I proposed that all my R.A.P. units stationed in Turin and the aliquots of forces already concentrated in Bra (about 600 men from the G.N.R. of the Turin and Cuneo Black Brigades and the Leonessa Armoured Group) take part in the operation. I also asked for the contribution of at least one battalion of the X Mas reinforced by an artillery group (on 2 btr.). The requests were entirely satisfied and I was granted the necessary vehicles and fuel to transfer the forces from Turin to the area of employment*'. As can be seen in the report, Zerbino granted Ruta all the vehicles and fuel necessary to transfer the troops from Turin to the zone of employment; this is a sign of the importance that the liberation of Alba held for the Republican authorities, given that it was very difficult to obtain petrol for the vehicles.

Initially, the attack was planned for 1 November and was to envelop Alba from all sides, developing as follows, according to the description of the plan devised by the colonel: '*Attack the northern side of the built-up area of Alba, crossing the Tanaro river by force; circumvent and destroy, with pincer action, the adversary forces stationed at the defence of the eastern and south-eastern outlets of the built-up area itself, acting with three attack columns:*

a) North Column - task: frontally attack the built-up area of Alba passing the Tanaro river with the largest forces on the Mussotto footbridge and with daring elements swimming and on floats penetrate the built-up area from the Tanaro gate and the Cherasco gate.

b) East Column - task: occupy with armoured elements the road junction near C. Sansoldo and with fire elements Q. 306 and Q. 33, south-west of Alba. Proceed successively: 1) with the largest forces for Q. 306, C. Fantina on the Alba Cortemilia road near C. Daniele, penetrating into the town from Savona gate; 2) with an aliquot of armoured vehicles, reinforced by infantry, reach Cherasco gate to support the action of the north column.

c) *South-West Column - task: occupy with fire elements Q. 253 of Villa Miroglio, proceed to the conquest of the two south-west outlets of the town of Alba, acting with the largest forces for the Roddi-Alba road axis*

The North column consisted of the I R.A.U., a platoon of the II R.A.U., a 75/13 Battery and two machine gun sections of the X Special Artillery Group, two 47/32 cannons and two 81 mortars; the East column consisted of the II R.A.U., a second 75/13 Battery of the X Special Artillery Group, two protected vehicles and one radio station. Finally, the South - West column was made up of the Turin and Cuneo Black Brigades, a G.N.R. Company, a platoon of the X MAS, with the support of an M13/40 tank of the 'Leonessa' and 1 radio station. The attack march was to be coordinated by the Command, which kept at its disposal for possible reinforcements a 105 Battery of the "Decima" and a Cavalry Platoon, while the three Columns were to reach Canale together, following the Turin - Moncalieri - Poirino - Pralormo - Montà- Canale itinerary, and then from there each was to follow different routes:

- the North Column was to stand in the Mussotto area;
- the East Column was to reach San Damiano d'Asti, from where it was to send a scouting party to see if it would be possible to cross the Tanaro river on the Motta bridge or by means of the Neive ferry. If neither option was feasible, he would have to cross the Tanaro at Asti, and then reach Asti, to operate the plan of attack previously reported;
- the South-West Column, having crossed the Tanaro at Mussotto, was to invest Alba on the side.

Monsignor Grassi himself, Bishop of Alba, recalls in his memoirs that '*Meanwhile, between 31 October and 1 November, huge Republican forces massed on the left bank of the Tanaro river from Pollenzo to Barbaresco; it was later learned that there were about three thousand soldiers with about twenty cannons stationed at various points, two armoured cars and several tanks*'.

On the morning of 1 November, the columns did indeed set off, but all the bridges over the Tanaro river, swollen due to the recent rains, had been interrupted and so the divisions had to deviate from their attack trajectories and stop at Bra, momentarily suspending the action; the planned route of march for the Eastern Column actually proved to be a very important tactical error, since, while the impossibility of crossing the Tanaro at the predetermined points must have been known, it was equally risky to reach Alba, passing through Asti, exposing the troops to a long movement in treacherous territory. Ruta thus had to revise and modify the original plan, scaling down the radius of action, now planned for the following day, 2 November, after having asked the Germans for permission to cross the Tanaro River at the Pollenzo bridge, a hamlet of Bra, which they were garrisoning, shifting the axis of the attack to the west side of the town of Alba.

In the meantime, the 'Lightning' Battalion of the 'Decima'[7] had arrived for further reinforcement, and a special department of the Fire Brigade of the Turin Provincial Command, which was equipped with airboats, had also reached the area.

---

[7] The 'Lightning' had been concentrated in Asti: the 2nd Company had arrived there on 31 October and the 3rd Company the following day. During the night of 2 November, on board trucks, the "Fulmine" moved towards Alba, reaching its destination with difficulty, due to the pouring rain.

At the stroke of midnight, Ruta issued the order to mobilise the approximately 3,000 Republican soldiers. Participating in the action were, in addition to the R.A.P. units more than 600 men from the Republican National Guard of Turin and Cuneo, the 1st Black Brigade 'Ather Capelli' of Turin, the 5th Black Brigade 'Carlo Lidonnici' of Cuneo, the 'Leonessa' Armoured Group, which provided support with 3 tanks and 2 armoured cars, a Battalion of Republican Police auxiliaries and the 'Lupo' (with its own L6/40 tank) and 'Fulmine' Battalions and the 'San Giorgio' Artillery Group, an artillery unit of the Decima Combat Group. During the operations, a mounted unit from Cuneo was also employed, whose organic dependency is unknown, and whose commander was Major Bonatelli.

At the time of the attack, the available forces were divided into three tactical groups:

1. The I R.A.U. and 1 Platoon of the II R.A.U., under the command of Lieutenant Colonel Berni, with the support of some 75/13 pieces of the X Special Artillery Group;
2. a training unit consisting of the 'Lupo' and 'Fulmine' Battalions of the Decima under the command of Lieutenant Commander Boriello;
3. a grouping formed by the units of the Black Brigades and the G.N.R., under the orders of Commander Ranza, with the support of Major Bonatelli's Cavalry Squadron.

On the opposite front, to the west was the 48th Garibaldi Brigade 'Dante Di Nanni', to the east was the 78th Garibaldi Brigade of Giovanni Rocca 'Primo', with the task of monitoring movements on the Tanaro river as far as Castagnole-Neive, to the south west were two detachments of the 'Castellino' Brigade of the I 'Langhe' Division. In direct defence of the built-up area to the north-east was the 'Alba' Brigade; further back, the autonomous partisans of the II 'Langhe' Division had placed two detachments of the 'Canale' Brigade in the second line to the east and, behind the hills, a detachment of the 'Belbo' Brigade. In reserve was Garibaldi's Michel detachment, 80 men strong. From the point of view of heavy armament, the partisan device had a section of 2 81 mm mortars from the "Val Tanaro" Brigade of the "Alpi" Division, under the command of Lieutenant Bologna, and a Heavy Weapons Unit of the 1st Alpine Divisions Group, armed with 4 13.2 mm machine guns, 4 81 mm mortars, 4 50 mm mortars and 4 British PIAT anti-tank bomb throwers.

According to Colonel Ruta's report, the partisan forces would total '*700 to 1,000 men in Alba; for the whole area from a minimum of 1,500 to a maximum of 5,000*', but, in reality, it was about 700 men in the city and the same number in the surrounding area.

At 1:00 a.m., about 600 R.S.I. soldiers, on board trucks with trailers, supported by some armoured vehicles, crossed the Pollenzo bridge, followed by another 'wave', while armoured vehicles of the Armoured Group 'Leonessa' stood by to support the fire where necessary. At 4:00 a.m., this grouping of Black Brigades and G.N.R. invested Alba from the southwest and east, reaching the town of Roddi (CN), which overran the partisans thanks to its numerical superiority, artillery support and the possibility of holding radio links between units. The units of the Decima reached the pre-established positions in two waves, due to a shortage of vehicles: first the "Lupo" Battalion was transported and the trucks, after unloading the men, had to turn back to transport the marines of the "Fulmine". At 6:00 a.m., according to Ruta's report, about sixty men from the R.A.U. and the "X" squadron were crossing the Tanaro on pneumatic boats downstream from Ponte Mussotto, vessels provided by the Piedmontese capital's Fire Brigade. At around 7:00 a.m. the combat group of the Decima MAS penetrated from Roddi, supported by the armoured vehicles of the "Leonessa", overtook the units of the G.N.R. and the Black Brigades, and in the meantime Case Alfieri and Villa Miroglio were hit with artillery fire, as heavy mortar fire was coming from there. The advance of the units of the "Lupo" Battalion was slowed down by a machine gun that had been installed by the partisans on the bell tower of Roddi, but they managed to flank the units of the I R.A.U.; the maroons were then divided into two groups, the 2nd Company continued the advance from the fields, while the 3rd from the surrounding hills. After noon, as the encirclement of the city was completed, extending the Republican troops' disposition also to the south, the Reparti Arditi and Decima units (to which the 'Lightning' Battalion had also finally rejoined) completely overran the city. The firefights lasted until 2 p.m., when the town was completely cleared of partisans. The partisans, disoriented by the impressiveness of the attacking forces and in any case fewer in number than those who conquered it[8], with connection and logistical difficulties (above all, the serious lack of ammunition), retreated and fell back into the hills. Colonel Ruta's report ends the mention of the clashes for the taking of Alba with these words: *'Having completed the investment of the city after repeated artillery concentrations, the columns of Arditi and the X penetrated Alba at 14.05 hours. A daring officer tore off the Savoy tricolour that the rebels had flown throughout the action on the city's highest bell tower'*. This is the description of the last fighting in a partisan document: *'After about an hour and a half of resistance on the 2nd line, most of the men being deprived of ammunition, the strongest automatic weapons having become unserviceable, I deemed it necessary to order a new retreat. In view of the men's discouragement at the lack of ammunition, the inconvenience to the weapons, the damage to the telephone line, and in order not to prolong the violent artillery fire on the city any longer and to save the organic efficiency of the divisions in order to be able to secure the areas behind; Considering that any further defence would have achieved only too slight a delay in the fall of the town and that in a defence that was too close entire divisions of ours could have been taken prisoner, I ordered the retreat on the displuvial line beyond the Cherasca valley, ordering the immediate clearing of the wounded, stores, prisoners, vehicles for which provisions had already been given since 8 a.m. of the same day"*.

The R.S.I. units had 4 dead and 10 wounded, while the partisans, according to the teletype sent to the Duce's Secretariat by Dr. Solaro, had 29 confirmed dead, 20 probable, and about 80 wounded. The republican dead were Sergeant Giovanni Pinon of the 3rd Company of the "Lupo" Battalion, sub-captain Sergio Franchi of the "Fulmine" Battalion, Captain Giovanni Consiglio and soldier Eustachio Aulitano of the "Ather Capelli" Black Brigade; the latter two died, killed by friendly fire, after being hit by mortar shells fired by the "Lupo" Battalion, which fell short due to the charges made damp by the inclement weather. Sub-Captain Franchi was decorated with the Silver Medal for Military Valour in his memory on 15 De-

---

[8] As the writer from Langhe Beppe Fenoglio wrote in his 'I ventitré giorni della città di Alba': *'Alba was taken by two thousand on 10 October and lost by two hundred on 2 November 1944'*.

cember⁹. The funeral services for the fallen were held in Turin on 4 November, during the celebrations for the anniversary of the victory in the First World War.

The number of partisan losses is quite confusing. In fact, Colonel Ruta's aforementioned report mentions 29 ascertained dead, 30 probable, 10 partisans passed away, about 80 wounded, 14 prisoners and 40 suspects captured. The Bishop of Alba, Monsignor Grassi, on the other hand, said in one of his letters: 'On the *subject of the dead, I must point out for the record that the Republican dead on 2 November were four and no more, just as there were four and no more partisans who died... Of the seriously wounded partisans, four were taken to the hospital and managed to escape, and no others are known to date.*

When operations were almost over, a Cavalry Squadron, with 60 horses, under the command of Captain Bussotti, arrived in Alba. He had been sent from the Army General Staff headquarters in Bergamo to take part in the operations and was then included in the Anti-Partisan Regiment. This was the first anti-partisan operation of a certain size conducted and commanded by Italians alone, who demonstrated a high degree of training in counter-guerrilla warfare. After the reoccupation of the city, the R.A.P. left the 2nd Battalion Arditi Fanti, the Cavalry Squadron from the Army General Staff and the 2nd 75/13 Battery of the 10th Special Artillery Group to garrison the city. On 12 November, the command of the city's garrison was entrusted to Lieutenant Colonel Pieroni, commander of the new Republican troops of the R.A.P., who had settled in Alba.

Bishop Grassi was taken to Turin, under arrest, on the charge of not having wanted to bless the bodies of the republicans who had died in Alba during the clashes, but, thanks to the intervention of the archbishop, he was immediately released, after receiving an apology from the Government High Commissioner Zerbino.

Following the fighting in Alba, the Ministry of the Armed Forces granted the Ardito badge to all soldiers who, employed in the fight against the 'rebels', had taken part in no less than three anti-partisan operations, through a resolution that gave the Chief of Staff of the Army the authority to issue the badges. In the Bulletin 'Note ed Informazioni per le Truppe Italiane' No. 2 of 20 December 1944, we read: 'The Ministry of the Armed Forces has ordered that the Ardito badge, instituted for soldiers belonging to the assault units of the previous world war, be extended to soldiers employed in the anti-rebel struggle and who have participated honourably in no less than three battles. The badge, entirely similar to the one established by circular No. 455 G.M. 1915, bears the motto "ITALIA" on the cross of the gladius and must be applied to the left sleeve of the jacket. Authorisation to wear the badge is granted by the Chief of Staff of the Army, who also issues the relevant patents. The Commanders of the anti-rebel troops will transmit monthly to the H.M.E. the list of soldiers who propose to be granted the badge'.

The republican authorities managed to maintain their garrison in the Piedmontese city from that moment on, also due to the fact that partisan activity during the winter of 1944-1945 was reduced to a minimum, only to resume the following spring.

---

9 This is the motivation: "*Sailor of ardent faith and indomitable spirit, struck dead by a mine blast that completely removed his lower limbs. Unconcerned by the pain, he incited his comrades to continue in their work of defending the homeland, declaring himself happy to sacrifice his youth for the common ideal. Transported to the hospital, his last words were dedicated to Italy and the Duce and he expired, once again invoking victory for Italian arms. Sublime example of conscious sacrifice, a warning to present and future generations*".

Appendix: Report of 'Captain Fede', commander of the Alba square, on the partisan defence of the city

"Italian National Liberation Army - Defence Command of the City of Alba
Benevello, 6 November 1944
Subject: Report on city defence operations.

Our situation
Deployment
Our deployment is framed to the west by the 48ª Garibaldi Brigade, which reaches with its deployment as far as the Cantina del Bivio di Roddi, to the east by the Garibaldi Brigade of Rocca, which has the task of monitoring movements on the Tanaro river as far as Castagnole-Neive. In order to ensure the suture to the west and recognising the need for a heavy weapon in the direction of Pollenzo, I ordered the dispatch of a 13.2 machine gun to the Rupe di Roddi detachment, while I invited "Kin"[10] commander of the 48ª Brigade to reinforce the Verduno-Roddi area with two other detachments with a total of 80 men, which our own Command would move by transmitting its order.
Our line-up is as follows:
Safety Zone: includes the following stop positions:
Casa Rabaglio (Lt. Bologna) Villa Monsordo - La Bemardina - Cascina Biancardi - C. Gallinotta - Le Basse.
L.R.: 1ˢᵗ Sector Lt. Renzo
Gherlone Castle -S. Cassiano-meeting point of the Verduno Canal with the cart track coming from S. Cassiano.
Sector II - 'Pepe' [11]
Canal of Verduno as far as the confluence with the Tanaro river-right bank of the Tanaro as far as Barbaresco. In order to shorten the line of resistance given the limited number of forces available and to force the enemy to channel themselves into the strip of land beaten by the guns set up on the hills, the land in front of the north-west and north of the Resistance Line (on the attached map, the area marked in red) had been flooded, following research carried out at the competent bodies in the previous days.
Mine fields were set up in the non-floodable areas in front.
Reserve: Garibaldi detachment Michel with 5 squads (80 men).
Health Service: dressing station at the Cemetery. Clearance of injured persons at the Civil Hospital. Links:
By means of order-holders with each Sector Commander (to be sent by each Sector Commander to the Defence Command on first alert).
Telephone: according to the following scheme for the implementation of which I had given orders to Lt. Carletto on my arrival:
Command: S. Cassiano-Bernardina-Roddi
Command: Cascina S. Cristina (Sector Command 'Pepe') Barbaresco

---

[10] Marco Fiorina 'Kin', born in 1915 and former Lieutenant of the Frontier Guard. Commander of the 48ª Garibaldi Brigade 'Dante di Nanni'.
[11] Giuseppe Toso 'Pepe', class of 1898 and former veterinary captain.

Due to a lack of wire, the lieutenant in charge told me that it was not possible for him to complete the diagram requested: Roddi and the 'Pepe' Command remained unconnected.

Aircraft reporting:

In order to enable the Allied air force to detect the course of our lines, the forward posts were promptly provided with signal sheets, the laying of which had been given precise instructions.

Provisions for possible retreat:

Second line of resistance:

q. 253 a S.S.O. di Alba (S. di Villa Miroglio) - Villa Miroglio - Fornace a Nord di V. Miroglio -Cimitero -Canale di Verduno - to rejoin the first Resistance Line.

Resistance in the City:

From the day of my arrival, I ordered, for the defence to the bitter end of the city, the construction of barrages at the various access roads, commissioning Commander Michel for the west side and Lieutenant Renato[12] for the east side. This work was just begun on the eve of the battle on the east side.

News about the enemy.

Information indicated that the enemy had the following forces and intentions:

S. Vittoria area: two Btg. equipped with barges intended to force the river in the Pollenzo-Roddi area and invest the city from the west

Biglini area: two or three specialised companies - a mixed 75 and 105 artillery group - and mortar and 47 gun units. In the area: 10 armoured cars, some L. wagons. 1 M tank.

Area north of Costigliele: a strong unit of about 1,000 men with artillery is reported, probably intending to force the Tanaro on our right flank.

Operations:

From my direct observation and from information gathered from various sources after the battle, the course of operations was as follows:

Day l/II. At 11.15 p.m., the order was given for the start of operations.

Day 2. Around 1 a.m. the enemy crossed the secretly repaired Pollenzo bridge with 600 men on trucks with trailers and some armoured vehicles followed by a second battalion.

Further east, later and in an evidently diversionary action, a small unit (about 60 men) crossed on barges.

Enemy reconnaissance and scouting patrols, attracted by a glimmer of light, surprised a group of four men, probably members of a security patrol on the river, intent on playing cards on the ground floor of a house (information from S.Lt. Franchi of the Cuneo Black Brigade) and killed three of them due to their energetic reaction to the order to surrender, while a fourth managed to escape capture[13].

At first light, an enemy patrol (9 men) was spotted by our 13.2 machine gun, which opened fire on it. Fearing an encirclement, considering himself unprotected on the flanks since he felt no reaction from the elements that should have been there, he withdrew to Diano d'Alba after a vigorous firing action.

---

12 Renato Carenzi.

13 In the text 'Con i partigiani in Valbormida...' (with the partisans in Valbormida...), op. cit. in bibliography, it is stated that the three were shot near the chapel of San Antonio al Toetto. They belonged to the 48th Garibaldi Brigade and were:
- Franco Bocca 'Zoe', class of 1922, former airman and decorated with the Bronze Medal for Military Valour
- Amedeo Piero Bosio 'Falco', class of 1924, decorated with the MBVM
- Giuseppe Sottimano 'Beppe', class of 1923

At about 7.45 a.m. during my inspection when I arrived in the locality of San Cassiano on my way to Roddi I was stopped by a Garibaldino from Michel's unit (who was returning from a leave) who informed me that he had been stopped by a woman in the Roddi area who told him that there were some republicans who had got off a boat in the number of about 40 in the locality of Toetto.

I immediately sent a patrol in that direction to gather some precise information and ordered Michel's division to join me at Cascina S. Cassiano. At the same time, by phonogram I ordered the Garibaldini di S. Gallo (who had arrived there) to prepare for a counter-attack by taking up a link on the right with Michel's unit, which had arrived by truck and which I had ordered to stem the infiltration and possibly eliminate the landing head created in conjunction with the Garibaldini di S. Gallo.

At about 8.15 a.m., I make a telephone request to Commander Poli[14] for the deployment of the 200 men planned for immediate reinforcement. The commander tells me that he cannot send more than about forty men, whom he assures will arrive in a short time.

At about 8.30 a.m., I informed the Kin Brigade Commander stationed at Morra by phonogram of the counter-attack ordered, inviting him to take surprise action behind the infiltrating units.

Lacking information from Michel, hearing only a light firing action in the Mulino di Roddi region and having observed the cessation of the firing action by the 13.2 machine gun of Casa Biancardi, I assumed that the enemy action had been confined. I also informed the Command of my impression in order to hearten the civilians who were previously working on the defensive arrangement and who were now impressed, to return to the town.

Convinced that I had established the situation in the sector, I reached Villa Miraglio where I had set up headquarters and there I was informed that enemy elements were attacking the Bernardina. As reinforcements were delayed, the various firing centres, arranged on the hill, retreated until they reached Villa Miraglio.

With the elements of the squads that had fallen back there and the reinforcement elements of Commandant Poli that had arrived in the meantime, (12 o'clock) I reinforced the second line of resistance.

After about an hour and a half of resistance, as most of the men were out of ammunition and the strongest automatic weapons (two 13.2 machine guns and two 8 machine guns) were rendered useless, I deemed it necessary to order a new retreat.

In view of the fact that:

1) *The men were disheartened mainly by the lack of ammunition and the subsequent serious inconvenience to the weapons;*
2) *Only inadequate passive defence works had been carried out on the various access roads to the city;*
3) *Drumming enemy artillery fire beat our second line, our supply route, and damaged telephone communications;*
4) *In order not to prolong the violent artillery fire on the city.*

In order to safeguard the organic efficiency of the wards and secure the back areas with this.

---

14 Piero Balbo, born in 1916, famous for being the 'Northern' commander in Beppe Fenoglio's book 'Il Partigiano Johnny'.

Considering that any further defence would only have achieved too slight a delay in the fall of the town and that in a defence that was too close, entire divisions of ours could have been taken prisoner, I ordered the retreat to the displuvial line beyond Valle Cherasca, ordering the immediate clearing of the wounded, stores, prisoners, vehicles, for which forecast provisions had already been given up to 8 o'clock that day. The following morning the divisions, on their own initiative, after being informed, roughly reached their starting positions.

The battle from April 1945 and the fall of the city

Between March and April 1945 there was an incredible escalation in the intensity of clashes between partisans and republicans, in which R.S.I units stationed in Alba often took part. Between 21 and 23 March, the 2nd Battalion of the R.A.P. Arditi, with the support of some wagons from the Nucleo Esplorante, carried out a combing around Alba, together with other republicans, during which eight partisans were killed, about forty suspects were captured and eighteen draft dodgers were arrested. On 24 March, the cavalry unit of the R.A.P. was attacked by Partisans while on patrol in the hills above Villa Gavuzzi and four soldiers were wounded during the attack.

Between 14 and 15 April, the partisans, aided by a parachuted British commando, surrounded and attacked Alba hard, in what, according to Monsignor Grossi, was the dress rehearsal for the city's liberation. A partisan document shows that the planned objectives for the action were very clear.

A large number of units took part in the attack for a total of about 600 men, 200 men of the 3rd and 10th 'Justice and Freedom' Division, 300 partisans of the 'Belbo' Brigade - 2nd 'Langhe' Division - and 100 men of the 21st Matteotti 'Fratelli Ambrogio' Brigade. In support of these were also the commando of the "Canuck" Mission, commanded by Captain Robert "Buck" MacDonald, about fifty men strong from 2nd Special Air Service armed with a 75 mm cannon, ten 3-inch mortars and a few .303 Vickers and .50 Browning machine guns.

To prevent a republican intervention from the neighbouring areas, the IX Garibaldi Division 'Alarico Imperito' was ordered to attack the republican garrisons of Canelli and Nizza, while the VI 'Asti' Division and the XII 'Bra' Division were to prevent the arrival of reinforcements from the two cities.

The action was preceded by the entry into the city at 3 a.m. of several groups of saboteurs who were to hit the Republican connection centres and form a stronghold within the city. At 6.30 a.m. the partisan attack started in three columns:

1. The first, made up of the 1st Detachment and the 'Belbo Brigade' guastatore platoon and elements of 'Giustizia e Libertà' under the orders of commander Gildo Fossati 'Gildo' was to attack on Villa Mancaretto and Fornace;
2. The second composed of the 3rd Detachment of the 'Belbo Brigade' and a 'Matteotti' detachment under the orders of commander Luigi Bezzuti 'Gino' attacked on Case Pericca;
3. The third formed by the 2nd Detachment of the 'Belbo Brigade' under the command of commander Franco Marchelli 'Marco' proceeded towards the railway bridge over the Tanaro river.

After 15 minutes of preparatory fire from MacDonald's unit - deployed on the heights southeast of Alba, the partisan units were to proceed with the elimination of all obstacles in their advance sector, but within 45 minutes at most, if the breakthrough manoeuvres were not successful, the partisan forces were to disengage. The partisan action actually unfolded according to the established plan and seemed to be on the verge of success, mainly due to the action of the 1st and 3rd columns, which rejoined around 10:30 a.m. and occupied three quarters of Alba, while the 2nd column had to retreat due to intense republican fire.

Despite the strenuous resistance of the Republican forces, until noon on the 15th the military garrison of the city seemed on the verge of capitulation.

In the Piedmontese town at that time, the R.A.P. deployed the 2nd Battalion Arditi Fanti, the 2nd Battery of the 10th Special Artillery Group (it is not clear whether armed with 75/13 howitzers or 75/27 cannons, as sources differ), a Cavalry Platoon and a section of 3 L3 light tanks, for a total of 487 men. The plan for the defence of the city by the Republican garrison hinged on 3 strongholds within the city:

- the Minor Seminary, where the Headquarters and the 5th Company of the 2nd Battalion of the R.A.P. Arditi Fanti, the 1st Section of the 2nd Battery of the 10th Special Artillery Group, commanded by Lieutenant Petrelli, and the armoured nucleus of the 1st Light Tank Company, deployed in the city, were concentrated;
- the Convitto Civico (Civic Boarding School), where the 8th Company of the 2nd Battalion Arditi Fanti was located, armed with 6 mortars and numerous heavy and light machine guns;
- the Govone Barracks, where the 1st Section of the 2nd Battery of the 10th Special Artillery Group, the staff of the Garrison Office and the Platoon of the Autonomous Cavalry Squadron had settled, but without their mounts, which had been moved to another building in the city.

Alba's external defence was articulated on a series of five garrisons, called 'blocking posts', placed at the city gates, whose task was to form a sort of belt around the town:

- Porta Cherasca (Autonomous Cavalry Squadron): hit by an intense attack from the beginning of the partisan offensive, it resisted without losses until 12 noon, when it received the order to retreat to the Minor Seminary;
- Porta Piave (Artillery); fell back at the beginning of the fighting, early in the morning, on the Govone barracks;
- Porta Vivaro (5th Company): was evacuated by the Command as early as the night of the 14th, due to its practically indefensible position;
- Porta Tanaro (8th Company): was immediately hit by a violent attack, as it was exposed to the huge mass of partisans concentrated on the banks of the Tanaro river. The blockade post, commanded by second lieutenant Saviano, had to fall back towards the Govone barracks, already around 7 a.m., after having lost 2 non-commissioned officers and 2 ardites;
- Porta Savona (5th Company): commanded by Second Lieutenant Pierani, was hit by the partisan attack at half past six. Shots from grenade launchers and Bren machine guns, fired from close range, damaged the defensive positions, which had been

set up, allowing the partisans to surround the blockhouse, where the Republican soldiers were barricaded. After unsuccessfully asking the republicans to surrender three times, the partisans sent two parliamentarians to negotiate, but Lieutenant Pierani, despite being seriously wounded in several parts of his body, refused to surrender his weapons. The partisans then resumed the attack with greater intensity; at this point, Pierani evacuated the civilians from the block of flats where he and his men of the 2nd Battalion of the Arditi were stationed, at the same time leaving the command to Corporal Magni, due to the seriousness of his wounds. At around 11.45 a.m., the partisans again sent two civilians to parliament: after more than five hours of fierce fighting, the 12 Republican soldiers were at the point of exhaustion and, after a brief negotiation, they decided to surrender, with the guarantee that their lives would be saved.

The partisan attack was intense and prolonged and, with the fall of the Porta Savona checkpoint, the situation was becoming increasingly critical for the Republican armed forces: let us now analyse the situation of the three strongholds.

Around noon, the partisans sent a request for surrender to the Govone barracks, through the young horseman Ermete Amadini, who had been taken prisoner together with a comrade and all the quadrupeds of the Autonomous Cavalry Department, in the stables where the horses had been kept; the surrender was, however, refused.

The situation near the Minor Seminary was less difficult: after being subjected to intense fire from automatic weapons, British mortars and grenade launchers and 47 cannons, positioned on the hills, the Republican soldiers began a heavy bombardment in response, with 45 mortars and 75/13 cannons, fire that forced the partisans to retreat to safer positions.

The 8th Company, commanded by Captain Arturo Cingano, was also in great difficulty, so much so that at about 10.00 a.m. a rescue mission was sent in, made up of men from the Command Platoon and the 5th Company, who found an almost compromised situation and numerous wounded. The partisans, after occupying the overlooking Major Seminary, from which they beat the boarding school, where the 8th Company was barricaded, with intense and continuous fire, attempted to break through the republicans' defence. It was not until around 1 p.m. that the soldiers of the 2nd Battalion Arditi managed to rebalance the situation, at least in part.

However, the intervention of the II R.A.U., which came to the rescue from Turin with the support of an L3 tank, was decisive. Assisted by the L tank of the Armoured Company, the officers attempted to attack the partisan forces from the outside, fording the Tanaro river. The manoeuvre, similar to the one carried out in the autumn, served to break the encirclement of the partisans, who were thus put to flight. However, the L3 tank was lost in this attempt because it ran aground trying to ford the Tanaro river. From Bra, another column arrived, made up of men from the I Reparto Arditi Ufficiali, two Plotoni della "Decima", an artillery section, four L3 tanks, a scout car, a scout motorcyclist and an R.F.5 radio station. An L3 tank from the city garrison became stuck due to skirmishing, while patrolling the perimeter of Alba; the vehicle was soon surrounded by partisans, the tank leader, second lieutenant Vari, got out of the tank, opening the way by firing his pistol, and attempted to return to the barracks, but, blocked by other partisans, was mortally wounded in the face.

The driver of the tank, corporal Cacciotti, took refuge in a house, was soon caught and shot. It was not until around 5 p.m. that the republican armed forces completely regained control of the situation and were able to start combing the entire town centre in search of any remaining partisan nuclei.

At the end of the I R.A.U.'s report, concerning the events of 15 April, we read that *'Towards dusk, it could be established that the garrison in Alba had barricaded itself in the two barracks and that the rebels, with the arrival of the column on the spot, were retreating, completely evacuating the town'*. Undoubtedly, the arrival of the Republican reinforcements was decisive, but the decision to exclude from the operation the Garibaldian formations present in the area, an exclusion strongly desired by the allied commands, also weighed on the outcome of the partisan attack. In the absence of these two conditions, in all probability, the partisan armed forces would have succeeded in the enterprise and would have occupied and held Alba until the end of the war. The operation proved, in any case, to be a success from a tactical point of view and also demonstrated the good level of efficiency achieved by the Resistance in managing the links between the different units deployed.

The Republican forces present in Alba recorded the following losses on that day: 8 dead, 17 wounded and 17 missing. Specifically, the fallen were:

- 5th Company
    - bold Mezzetti Giacomo
    - Lieutenant Moltrer Mario
- 8th Company
    - Sergeant Carrino Norberto
    - Lance Corporal Colombo Enrico
    - Sergeant Martini Egidio
    - bold Pedrali Giulio
- Tank Section
    - Corporal Cacciotti Gabriele
    - Second Lieutenant Vari Ardenio

Partisan losses were five killed and 16 wounded, and specifically the casualties were:

- Belbo' Brigade
    - Valerio Boella 'Walter'
    - Marcello Montersino 'Job'
    - Romano Scagliola 'Diaz'
- X 'Justice and Freedom' Division
    - Albino Mereu 'Albino'
    - Oronzo Solazzo 'Oronzo'

Following this episode, the military presence of the Anti-Partisan Regiment in Alba was reinforced, with the 3rd Battalion of Alpine Ardites also deployed in the city.

However, events were now precipitating: having broken through the Gothic Line, the Allies were spreading into the Po Valley. The garrison in Alba was again attacked on 26 April and the Republican garrison surrendered after two days of resistance to the attacks by the partisans of the II 'Langhe' Division and the 21st Matteotti Brigade; after surrendering, the soldiers suffered the partisans' anger. The partisan formations, however, quickly overran the city: after eighteen months of clandestine fighting, the guerrillas aimed decisively at the large cities that were already in upheaval. Major Gagliardo Gagliardi, commander of the 2nd Battalion Arditi Fanti, and Captain Amleto Rossi, commander of the 5th Company of the same Battalion, were put on trial on 30 April 1945 and shot on 2 May at the cemetery in the same town of Alba.

Appendix: the report on the battle of 15 April 1945, written by the commander of the 2nd Battalion Arditi Fanti of the R.A.P.

In order to delve deeper into the unfolding of the events that characterised the attack that the partisan forces carried out on the Republican garrison of Alba, we reproduce the full text of the report written by Major Gagliardo Gagliardi, commander of the 2nd Battalion of the Arditi Fanti Anti-Partisan Regiment. We considered it appropriate to reproduce the text of this document, as it recounts in great detail how the events unfolded, underlining how the R.S.I. forces found themselves in difficulty for long hours, so much so that they were on the verge of capitulation several times. In the chapter dedicated to the units deployed in Alba on that fateful 15 April 1945, the reports of the commanders of the individual companies of the II Battaglione Arditi Fanti and the commander of the Sezione Carri Armati. are also included, providing a detailed view of each unit employed in the battle.

"II BATTALION ARDITI R.A.P.
COMMAND
No. 218/OP of prot.
P.o.C. 841 on 20 April 1945/XXIII

Subject: Resistance of the Alba Military Presidium to the partisan attack on 15 April 1945.

To the R.A.P. Command
P.o.C. 841

On the evening of 14 April, a trustworthy information source reported that during the night of the 15th, partisans would attempt to occupy the town of Alba.
Early reports indicated a large gathering of outlaws, about a thousand, in the hamlet of Gallo, about 9 km from Alba.
Further reports indicated heavy massing on the heights surrounding the Presidium, with a prevalence in the Madonna di Como area.
I was in charge of issuing orders to the department commanders and setting up the defences for each provision and checkpoint.
A Section of Artillery, commanded by S. Lt. Pedrelli Eugenio, moved to the Minor Seminary's basement, while the Cavalry, fully manned, retreated to the Govone Barracks, leaving the quadrupeds with their guards in the stables.
The Presidium was thus established on three strongholds:

Minor Seminary: 5th Company, Headquarters, Armoured Core and Artillery Section set aside;
Civic boarding school: provisioning of the 8th Company;
Govone Barracks: Artillery Section, Foot Cavalry, Presidio Office staff
as well as four roadblocks, having folded the one on Via Vivaro, which was less well defended due to its unfavourable position.

At each stronghold, the Department Commanders set the platoons the defence sectors, reinforcing the automatic weapon emplacements and consequently guarding the emplacements themselves.

The night passed calmly.

At dawn, around 6 a.m., the three men of the Command Platoon, on duty at the Automatic Telephone Exchange, spotted a time bomb in front of the main door of the Exchange, which they blew up, causing alarm at the Presidium and foreshadowing the attack that had been set by the enemy with the bursting of the device.

At 6.12 a.m., on the enemy side, the attack began with intense artillery fire, automatic, light and heavy weapons, which simultaneously hit the strongholds.

The opposing forces were thus dislocated:

Tanaro river sector (on the right bank);
Hills facing Porta Cherasca;
Madonna della Moretta (near Cascina Miroglio);
Zonda of the Alba Cemetery.

The enemy, exploiting weak points in the defence, penetrated the city from Via Vivaro and Istituto S. Paolo.

Due to damage caused to the S.T.I.P.E.L., connections between the strongholds completely failed; later, at 7.50 a.m., a radio failure cut off communication with the Higher Command.

Roadblock resistance.

Porta Cherasca (service performed by the detachment of the Autonomous Cavalry Squadron). The checkpoint at the beginning of the attack was hit by an intense fire of automatic weapons, placed in positions near the mill and in the neighbouring blockhouse. The enemy, attempting to neutralise the defence, placed a grenade launcher close to the stronghold, seriously damaging it; nevertheless, the service personnel managed to rearrange the automatic weapons and concentrate their fire on the shooter of the grenade launcher, who was eliminated. Subsequent attacks were valiantly repulsed and the position was held, without losses, until 12 noon, when the 5th Company was ordered, by relay, to fall back into the 5th Company's reserves.

Porta Savona (service performed by a squad from the 5th Company). At about 6.30 a.m., the attack against the checkpoint began at close range. Six shots from grenade launchers dismantled the defensive preparations of the stronghold from the first minutes.

The enemy, supported by Bren machine-gun fire from both the Viale della Moretta and the Ferrovia gully, managed to surround the blockhouse. Three summonses to surrender were sent to our men: the responses were machine-gun fire and individual weapons.

The rebels, seeing the futility of their efforts, sent two burghers to negotiate: S. Lt. Pierani

Giovanni, commander of the checkpoint, wounded in the groin, both thighs and one arm, continued to incite the men and refuse to surrender.

At the exhortation of some of the inhabitants of the block of flats to desist from the unequal fight, the officer replied that he was a man of honour and would not give in as long as he had ammunition.

The partisans blew up the gate with plastic mines and threw themselves down the stairs: one was stabbed by one of our daring men, another fell riddled with bullets; the enemy fell back with several wounded.

The fire flared up again; S. Lt. Pierani accepted that the civilians were evacuated from the barracks and with his men helped them to safety.

Further demands for surrender were made with the threat that they would blow up the blockhouse with dynamite: the response was always negative.

S. Lt. Pierani, no longer able to lead the men due to physical impossibility, gave the direction of the stronghold to Corporal Magni.

At 11.45 a.m., after more than five hours of resistance, a band leader, a certain Mario, sent two civilians to parliament; S. Lt. Pierani, who had been left with four magazines, declared that he would speak only on the condition that the partisan presented himself to him unarmed, which he accepted, presenting himself in a rigid posture of greeting and praising him with all the soldiers who had honourably resisted in twelve against more than two hundred.

The commander of the checkpoint asked:
- honour of arms for all men;
- intangibility of people;
- continue to wear the uniform of the Republican army and remain united in the camp;
- adequate nourishment of the same.

Having accepted these conditions from both sides, Lieutenant Pierani emerged from the blockade post at the head of his men, armed and in perfect order, and marched in front of the enemy to the corner of Via S. Paolo, at which point the men laid down their weapons, while the officer kept his pistol.

The partisan leader who had signed the surrender and the commander of the operation in Alba, congratulated the officer and supported him on his wounds that prevented him from walking.

Porta Piave (service disengaged by the artillery), given the location of this checkpoint the members fell back at the first sight of fire to the Govone barracks.

Porta Vivaro (service performed by the 5th Company), as previously mentioned, this checkpoint was unmanned on the evening of the 14th.

Porta Tanaro (service carried out by the 8th Company), the situation at the checkpoint was in a precarious state given the large number of partisans who attempted to occupy it from the banks of the Tanaro, subjecting it to violent fire from automatic weapons and grenade launchers.

At around 7 a.m., the personnel, under the command of S. Lt. Saviano, began the retreat, returning to the camp with the following losses:
- sergeant A.U. Carrino Norberto
- bold Pedrali Giulio

- bold Benedetti Giuseppe
- U.S. Sgt. Martini Egidio
- Daring Dotti Constantine

The two non-commissioned officers were captured near the Piazza del Duomo and subsequently slaughtered with a shot to the back of the head, while Pedrali, the heavy machine-gun carrier, was mortally wounded.

Dotti, who had been shot in both legs, was later found at the local civil hospital, where he was transported by a non-commissioned officer of the Alba fire brigade, a certain Roggiero; Benedetti, on the other hand, was able to reach the hospital, although he was shot in the lumbar region.

Headquarters Govone Barracks:
- arranged to defend themselves, the service personnel tenaciously repelled the attacks, while the artillery section and the cavalry mortar beat the points where the adversary's concentration was most noticeable.

The situation, which was already worrying due to the intense enemy fire, was becoming more critical due to the continuous adversary siege, exacerbated by the fall of the Savona Gate checkpoint and the absolute lack of connections.

At around 12 o'clock, Amadini Ermete, a cavalry balkie (who, together with another comrade, had been captured in the stables where the cavalry's quadrupeds were kept, quadrupeds taken by the partisans), called for the surrender of the outlaws, which was decisively refused, despite being told that all the garrison's forces had been overwhelmed and destroyed. The Balilla, invited to remain in the barracks, replied that he had given his word of honour to return and also to save his comrade who was threatened with execution if he failed to return.

The first news reached the stronghold, when an 'L' tank was able to reach it at around 4 p.m., at which time the enemy pressure was reduced.

For the entire duration of the attack, the Govone barracks was subjected not only to automatic weapons fire, but also to the firing of incendiary grenades and 45 mortar bombs.

There were two light casualties:
art. Caprino Mario, caval. Gherardi Angelo.

The Autonomous Cavalry Squadron lost, in addition to the two captured soldiers, Cav. Amadini Ermete and Can. Polloni Silvio, 36 horses, two mules, a wagon luggage all the saddlery material, 3 muskets.

Men and materials, these, who were not part of the Govone stronghold.

Minor Seminary and Civic Boarding School

From the very first minutes of fire from the 5th Company's positions, a precise and well-aimed automatic weapons fire started, containing the adversary on the right bank of the Tanaro, inflicting considerable losses so much so as to make him desist from the intention of investing the provision and allowing the personnel of the Porta Tanaro blocking post to fall back.

The enemy fire pounded the barracks courtyard, making it difficult for the artillery pieces to manoeuvre and for the tanks to come into action.

At around 7 a.m., the encampment was subjected to bombardment by British grenade launchers, 55 mortars, and 47 guns that were placed on the Cherasca hills.

This fire could be countered with 45 mortars and 75/13 pieces, forcing the opponent to abandon the fight.

The situation of the 5th Company began to normalise, while that of the 8th Company, located in the Civic Boarding School, became precarious, so much so that around 10 am, two squads, one from the 5th Company and one from the Command Platoon, came out of the Minor Seminary to see what was happening. On this occasion, Lieutenant Doctor Colucci Amedeo went to the headquarters of the 8th Company to give first aid to several wounded, including the Commander, Capt. Cingano Arturo, who was wounded in several parts after a grenade launcher had exploded; while Engineer Bruno joined the teams to search for a civilian radio fitter to repair the radio equipment that was not in a condition to be able to transmit with the Higher Command.

The Major Seminary, whose façade overlooks the courtyard of the Civic College, was occupied by a strong core of partisans who subjected the courtyard itself to intense automatic weapons fire, thus neutralising the use of the 81 mortars that were placed in the courtyard to pound the areas in front of the checkpoints.

The situation, made more critical by the continuous advance of the enemy who attempted to occupy the premises of the boarding school, passing through the adjacent church, led to the retreat of the entire company to the entrance hall, which was subjected to concentric grenade-throwing fire.

Towards 1 p.m., having succeeded in putting the two heavy machine guns and an 81 mortar into operation, with the sacrifice of the life of Capt. Maj. Colombo Enrico, who had volunteered to remove it from the courtyard, the building where the partisans were stationed, came to be heavily beaten to such an extent that the situation of the 8th Company was partly normalised.

The squad of the Command Platoon, escorting the Doctor, returned to Seminario Minore, while the squad of the 5th Company, commanded by Lt. Marquez Giovanni, attempted to search for the radio-mounted soldier and then went to the Govone Barracks.

In the centre of the city, this squad was hit by Bren and Sten volleys from adversary nuclei stationed in dwellings, so much so that it was impossible to continue the task, even suffering two casualties: Geniere Bruno Giovanni, Capt. Porro Luigi.

Lieutenant Marquez arranged to defend himself in a block of flats by barricading the access roads and clearing it of civilians. Later spotted by partisan squads, who demanded his surrender, he refused, hitting the adversary with individual weapon fire, causing the death of four outlaws.

The squad disengaged around 5 p.m., when the pressure was completed, reaching the Govone Barracks and raking the first suburbs of the city.

A Platoon of the 5th Company, under the command of Lt. Moltrer Mario, around 2 p.m., at the request of the 8th Company commander, attacked the Major Seminary from behind, in order to definitively dislodge the enemy nucleus stationed there. The task was carried out, the Platoon returned in full after having combed the entire area.

At about 4 p.m., due to the pressing call for help from the Company, which was once again besieged in its provisions, Lieutenant Moltrer Mario's Platoon came to the rescue. Near Piazza del Duomo, four enemy grenades suddenly arrived, hitting the Platoon and Lieutenant

Moltrer Mario was killed along with Bersagliere Mezzetti Giacomo, while Lieutenant Giliberti Pietro's lower limbs were wounded.

From the early hours of the morning, two 'L' wagons attempted to reach the Govone Barracks and bring help to the checkpoints, in order to allow them to fall back; of the two wagons, only one returned, reporting that it had only been able to reach Piazza Savona, where it had been fired upon by a large number of individual automatic weapons to which it was unable to react due to the momentary inefficiency of the weapons on board. Plastic mines had been placed along the road.

The other tank, due to a track failure, became stuck; the crew, composed of S. Lt. Vari Ardemio and Capt. Maj. Cacciotti Gabriele, exited the tank to carry out the repair. As the officer was lowered in an attempt to put it back into working order, he was mortally wounded and the graduate, with his right hand clearly removed, repaired to a civilian home, where he was given first aid. When spotted, he responded to an order to surrender by throwing a hand grenade that killed two partisans.

Subsequently captured, and in an unresisting condition, he was slaughtered.

Around 5 p.m., the general situation began to normalise, so much so that the two tanks and a few platoons were deployed to comb the town of Alba.

By now the enemy had fallen back, having heard of the immediate arrival of reinforcements, and about an hour later it could be said that the area around the city had been cleared.

At 11 p.m., the first radiogram was sent to the Higher Command so that reinforcements could arrive the following morning.

The night passed calmly.

Overall, the action resulted in the following losses:

Dead: 2 Officers, 2 NCOs, 4 Troops
Injured: 3 Officers, 2 NCOs, 12 Troops (two serious)
Missing: 1 Officer, 1 NCO, 15 Troops
Quadrupeds: 36 horses, 2 mules.

Armament
2 heavy machine guns installed on the 'L' wagon
1 machine gun, at the Porta Savona checkpoint
5 automatic machine guns
6 guns
20 muskets mod. 91

Armament, mostly, in the hands of missing and deceased soldiers.

Various materials
The trousseau and equipment of the missing, a baggage wagon, all the saddlery equipment of the Autonomous Cavalry Squadron were lost.

Losses inflicted on the enemy

From information gathered, the partisan forces were led by British officers who had set up headquarters at Cascina Rocca and Cascina Giovin, in the hills east of Alba, and had set up two groups to rescue, sort and concentrate dead and wounded.

The first group at the Alba Cemetery sorted, among the dead and wounded, 74 people.

For the second centre, at Madonna degli Angeli, there are two differing versions, one setting the figure of those sorted at 208, while the second asserts that the group leader who directed the sorting reported the figure of 183 individuals.

Excluded from this count are those from the Tanaro sector that were sorted in the Mussotto area, those that fell into the Tanaro itself and those found on its banks.

In total, without fear of being mistaken, it can be said that the losses inflicted on the enemy amounted to around 150 dead and 300 wounded.

Material recovered

3 Vetterling rifles
6 complete magazines for Bren machine gun
1750 cartridges per said
13 magazines for Breda machine gun
8 British grenades
2 replacement barrels for Bren machine gun
1 rifle mod. 91
various magazines for weapons 91
30 S.I.PE. type bombs.

Troop behaviour: commendable.
Weather conditions: mild temperature and clear skies.

The Battalion Commander
Maj-Gen Gagliardo Gagliardi

▲Images of the funeral held in Alba on 3 September 1944 of two fallen 'Apennine Hunters' from the local Republican garrison (from 'Acta').

▼ Soldiers of the Republican National Guard and the Grenadier Battalion of the C.A.R.S. during the funeral ceremony (from 'Acta').

▲ The two fallen, Lieutenant Ragazzini of the 3rd G.N.R. Battalion and Grenadier Abiuso of the 1st 'Grenadiers of Sardinia' Battalion, had been shot in two separate ambushes (from 'Acta').

▼ The funeral cortege leaves Alba Cathedral (from 'Acta').

▲ Alpine soldiers of the 'Cadore' Battalion during their stay in Piedmont. The 'Cadore' had been attached to the Centro Addestramento Reparti Speciali (Special Forces Training Centre), to be used in the anti-partisan struggle and had been placed to garrison the city of Alba (Archive 'Monterosa' Division).

▲ Partisan commander Enrico Martini known as 'Mauri', one of the architects of the occupation of Alba and the establishment of the Partisan Republic.

▼ Partisans in the town of Alba, after the abandonment of the Social Republic garrison.

▲ Partisan vehicles from Commander Mauri's bands in Alba, during the period of the 'Republic of Alba'. In the foreground, a FIAT 508 and a FIAT 626 truck, presumably both stolen from German units; on the right, a tanker truck on a Lancia 3 RO can be glimpsed (Manes).

▲ Mauri, centre with a Thompson submachine gun, in conversation with some partisans in Piazza Savona in Alba immediately after the entry of Resistance forces into the city in October 1944 (Manes).

▲ A group of soldiers from the Reparti Arditi Ufficiali during a counter-band action: the men of the I and II R.A.U. were among the protagonists of the Alba shooting on 2 November 1944 (Gallesi).

▼ A squad of R.A.U. officers during a combing action in Piedmont; interestingly, the first on the left is carrying a 45 mm Brixia assault mortar (Gallesi).

▲ Other elements of the same department of the Reparti Arditi Ufficiali in Piedmont: they all wear special camouflage clothing, made from Italian M29 fabric and have automatic weapons, suitable for close combat (Gallesi).

▼ An L3 light tank of the Anti-Partisan Regiment supports elements of an Arditi Ufficiali Division in Piedmont (Gallesi).

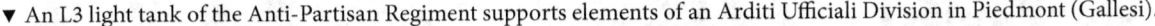

▲ A photograph, from the same series as the previous ones, depicting a soldier of the Arditi Ufficiali with the camouflage suit, distributed to the Arditi to operate more safely during counter-guerrilla operations (Gallesi).

RICEVUTO PER TELESCRIVENTE

SSS MADERNO DA TORINO 2073 207 2 2300
- ENTE AUTORIZZATO -
PREFETTO TASSINARI SEGRETERIA DEL DUCE MADERNO

STAMANE DOPO FATICOSA PREPARAZIONE DOVUTA TOTALE MANCANZA PONTI SUL TANARO SI EST INIZIATA NOTA AZIONE DOPO PREPARAZIONE ARTIGLIERIA ET TRAGHETTO TANARO LA CITTA' DI ALBA EST STATA CONQUISTATA ASSALTO VERSO ORE 14 REPARTI PARTECIPANTI BRIGATA NERA DI CUNEO BRIGATA NERA CAPELLI DI TORINO REPARTO CORAZZATO LEONESSA DELLA GNR REPARTO DELLA GNR DI TORINO ET CUNEO BATTAGLIONE LUPO FULMINE ET GRUPPO ARTIGLIERIA DELLA DECIMA MAS REPARTI DELL'ESERCITO REPUBBLICANO ET ARDITI UFFICIALI TORINO COMANDANTE MILITARE DELL'AZIONE TENENTE COLONNELLO RUTA PERDITE TRE MORTI DUE CAPELLI TORINO DI CUI UN UFFICIALE UNO DELLA DECIMA MAS DIECI FERITI DI CUI CINQUE DELLA DECIMA MAS DUE CAPELLI TORINO DUE REPARTI ARDITI UFFICIALI UNO LEONESSA GNR GIORNI PRECEDENTI IN RICOGNIZIONE UN CADUTO ET DUE FERITI DI CUNEO RISULTATI CONQUISTA DELLA CITTA' OCCUPATA DA OLTRE MILLE DEL GRUPPO MAURE MUNITI DI ARMI PESANTI ET MORTAI RIBELLI UCCISI 29 ACCERTATI SUL POSTO ET 20 INDIVIDUI RIBELLI FERITI CIRCA 80 CATTURATI UNA DECINA L'ALTRI IN FUGA DISORDINATA SONO ENTRATI IN CITTA' CON CAMERATI ZERBINO GALLARDO RONZA LAMATTI POLVANI FIANELLI GORI TEALDI ET ALTRI COMANDANTI AD ALBA ABBIAMO FATTO ISSARE SU CAMPANILE GAGLIARDETTO NERO DELLA RIVOLUZIONE PREGOTI RIFERIRE AL DUCE ENTUSIASMO DECISIONE FASCISTI PIEMONTESI

-DELEGATO PIEMONTE DOTTOR SOLARO -

▲ Teletype with which the Turin Federal Commissioner Giuseppe Solaro announced to Prefect Tassinari, of the Duce's Special Secretariat, the recapture of Alba by Republican forces on 2 November 1944.

Allegato n°5

REPARTI CHE HANNO PARTECIPATO ALLA LIBERAZIONE DI ALBA
NEI GIORNI 31 OTTOBRE - 3 NOVEMBRE 1944/XXII

	Ufficiali	Sottufficiali e truppa	ARMI FANTERIA					ARTIGLIERIA			Anticarro	Mezzi protetti	Carri Armati	Autoblindo
			Mortai 81	Mortai 45	Pezzi da 47	Mitragliatrici	Fucili mitragliatori	75/13	105				
R.A.P.													
Comando	5	10											
1° R.A.U.	110	11	2		2		2						
2° R.A.U. (1 pl.)	50												
X Btr. Sp.	5	52				2	3	4					
Bat.Cav.	2	35											
Elementi genio	1	10											
Xª MAS													
Btg. LUPO	12	400	2	4	1	4	12						
" FULMINE	9	360				4	9	1					2
Btr. SAN GIORGIO	3	100								4			
Btr. DA GIUSSANO	2	100						4					
G.N.R. C.do Prov. Torino (compresi 11 elementi del Gr.Cor. Leonessa)	8	87	2			1	2			1		4 (L3) 1 (M13)	
G.N.R. C.do Cuneo	1	?				4	6						
Vigili Fuoco Torino	1	?											
Corpo Ausiliario B.N.	2	40											

▲ Transcription of a prospectus of the National Republican Army, which summarises the Republican units that took part in the fighting for the reoccupation of Alba at the beginning of November 1944. It is interesting to note that for each unit, not only the number of men, but also the details of the armament are indicated. The presence of two armoured cars for the 'Lightning' Battalion of the X MAS (which in reality only had a homemade armoured vehicle) is not clear, while there is no mention of the L6/40 tank of the 'Wolf' Battalion, which was photographed at the end of the fighting inside the Piedmontese town.

▲ A unit of a R.A.U. on the march during a combing action in Piedmont All soldiers wear 1929 model fabric camouflage combinations and have automatic weapons, suitable for close combat (Viziano).

▼ In order to move around safely in areas where the partisan presence was strongest, it was customary to keep a machine gun ready to fire on the roof of the truck cab, as in the case of this Lancia RO of probable civilian origin used by the Anti-Partisan Regiment. The vehicle is painted sand-coloured, camouflaged with small patches, probably green, and is armed with a Breda (Viziano) machine gun.

▲ Marines of the 1st Company of the "Lightning" Battalion of the Decima waiting to cross the Tanaro to take part in the fighting in Alba. They almost all wore the camouflage uniform, typical of the X MAS (Panzarasa) units.

▼ Some men of the 3rd Platoon of the 1st Company of the 'Lightning' Battalion photographed at the end of the fighting in Alba on 2 November 1944. In the centre with the envelope cap, the Platoon commander, Ensign Enzo Fumagalli, on whose right can be seen Mrs Ebe Orrù, wife of the Battalion commander Lieutenant Giuseppe Orrù (Panzarasa).

▲ Along this column, filmed in Piedmont in November 1944, one can see the artisanal armoured car of the 'Lightning' Battalion of the X MAS, which would also be used during the taking of Alba, but did not take part in the fighting (Panzarasa).

▼ L6/40 tank of the 'Lupo' Battalion of the X MAS, photographed at the end of the clashes with which the fascist forces retook the town of Alba at the beginning of November 1944; in the photograph, the tank appears without the 20 mm cannon.

▲ The Turin Black Brigade 'Ather Capelli' also took part in the operations in Alba in November 1944 with one of its contingents; pictured here is a platoon of Black Brigade squads in the summer of 1944.

▼ Elements of a Republican Police department during an anti-partisan operation in Piedmont in the autumn of 1944. The Turin Police Headquarters provided a Battalion of Auxiliaries during clashes in Alba (Arena).

THE SITUATION OF THE PARTISAN FORCES IN THE LANGHE FROM SUMMER 1944 TO MAY 1945

Autonomous Departments

In the spring of 1944, the autonomous detachments under the command of Enrico Martini Mauri suffered a very harsh razing in the Casotto, Maudagna and Mongia valleys that practically eliminated the Major's forces almost completely.

In April, Mauri decided to move to the Langhe and established that the first actions to be carried out in that area were sabotage, weapons recovery and hand-to-hand attacks, while in the event of an enemy attack, the units were to encircle and destroy the adversaries only if they were in small numbers.

As far as recruitment was concerned, Mauri put it in the hands of the group leaders, so that they could choose elements of sure loyalty, leaving out possible spies or infiltrators of the enemy.

In the Langhe, Mauri also managed to meet Ignazio Vian[15], who had retreated to Alba after the catastrophe in Val Corsaglia, and immediately began organising a new formation thanks to the action of Captain Icilio Ronchi Della Rocca[16] in Bra and Captain Franco in Alba.

During the month of April, Mauri's formation was still very small and carried out few actions, partly due to the drastic lack of ammunition and weapons.

Its units were structured as very agile flying squads that roamed the Langhe.

In the same month came the sad news of the arrest of Vian, who was on a mission in Turin and was captured thanks to the action of a spy. He was killed by hanging, after attempting suicide, on 22 July in Turin along with three other partisans and was later decorated with the Gold Medal for Military Valour.

In May, Mauri decided to find a stable base and with his 50 men reached an old farmstead in Igliano, which was used as a command post and defended by an entrenchment.

Already on 12 May, the formation received an attack from R.S.I. units thanks to the action of a spy who discovered Mauri's command.

Three columns of the Mobile Autonomous Legion 'Ettore Muti', led respectively by Alessandro Bongi, Luciano Folli and Ampelio Spadoni, attacked the partisans at 6.45 a.m., but the republicans did not expect the presence of an entrenchment and were thus caught off guard and - after having had two casualties[17] - retreated without inflicting any losses on the partisans.

---

15 A former second lieutenant of the Frontier Guard who *was* part of the *Boves Band*, which joined Mauri's forces after its destruction in February 1944.

16 Icilio Ronchi della Rocca, born in 1910, former captain of the artillery who operated in the Bra area immediately after the armistice

17 Mario Francesco Tedeschi, born in 1900, and Vito Diliberti, born in 1925 and former partisan from Ceva. Taken from M. Griner, "La "Pupilla" del Duce. La Legione autonoma mobile Ettore Muti", op. cit. in bibliography and from A. Conti, "Albo caduti e dispersi della Repubblica Sociale Italiana", op. cit. in bibliography

Between May and June, Mauri's unit increased its numbers to around 150 men, while from the beginning of June, precisely from 3/4, the first supplies also arrived from the Allied air force and paratroopers[18].

During this period, there were also organisational changes, in the Langhe Captain Franco took command of the formations near Alba, while Della Rocca retained command of those in the Braidese, and between the two operated a formation under the orders of Mario Lamberti[19].

In the Mangio area, a formation was set up thanks to the union of the forces of 'Poli' and 'Carletto' and finally, between Cherasco and Narzole, a plain formation was set up under the orders of Colonel Ferrero.

Formations in the valleys abandoned in March were also revived, 'Martinengo'[20] reconstituted a unit in Val Tanaro, Lieutenant Lulli[21] went to Val Corsaglia - but during a trip to Milan he was captured and interned so the command passed to Tozzi - while in Val Maudagna a unit was reconstituted from scratch under the orders of 'Giacomino'[22].

Mauri, together with the commanders of the various detachments, organised a general action, giving orders to strike and hold the Republican and German forces in various areas. The attack took place during the night of 11 June, the formation of 'Martinengo' reoccupied the forts of Col di Nava, those of Della Rocca and Franco interrupted the lines of communication between Bra and Alba, Marco blew up the railway between Bra and Turin, and finally, Pippo attacked Ceva but had to desist because of the tough resistance from the men of the 'Ettore Muti'.

In the meantime, Mauri, with his men, advanced towards Lesegno to recover his parents, who were in danger of being deported to Germany, and to capture the village mayor.

As soon as they arrived in the town, the men of the Mobile Autonomous Legion 'Ettore Muti' were dislodged and took refuge in the town's castle; in the clash, two militiamen were captured, a partisan deserter and four members of the Republican Fascist Party were killed, but the mayor was not captured, because his residence was well defended.

During the transfer to Cigliè Mauri managed to find Mario Bogliolo[23], who had disappeared since the March round-up and had fled to Liguria and then moved to the Como area.

As soon as he heard that Mauri had survived the round-up, he moved immediately to the Langhe.

---

18 Mauri states that the first were Gentile Francesco, mission leader, Scudeller Giovanni 'Leone' and Cingolani Marcello 'Marcellino', who were parachuted in with the HHH Mission on 3 June 1944. In reality, the first mission reached Cuneo and Mondovì in early February 1944, after having landed in Liguria; forming the 'Charterhouse' mission were Second Lieutenant Italo Cavallino Sirio, Second Lieutenant Nino Bellegrandi 'Annibale' and 1st Class Secondo Balestra Biagio. Taken from "Le missioni alleate e le formzioni dei partigiani autonomi nella Resistenza piemontese: atti del Convegno internazionale: Torino, 21-22 October 1978", op. cit. in bibliografia.
19 Class of 1915, former non-commissioned officer in the Regia Aeronautica.
20 Eraldo Hanau, born in 1905.
21 Folco Lulli, born in 1912, was commander of an irregular band during the Ethiopian War and then developed anti-fascist ideas. After the armistice he became a partisan in Mauri's formation, later being captured and deported by the Germans. After the war he became an actor and voice actor.
22 Giacomino Curreno 'Gimmy', born in 1928, escaped from the Regio Collegio 'Carlo Alberto' in Turin after the armistice and was killed in combat in March 1945.
23 Former marshal of the CCCI Battalion of Machine Gunners and detachment commander missing with his unit after the March 1944 round-up.

In the days following the attack, new volunteers flowed into *Mauri*'s formations, but this had also brought the unit to the attention of the Italo-Germans who, on the 21st, starting from Lesegno, attacked the partisan garrison in Castellino Tanaro held by 'Renzo's' men[24]. Mauri, in his memoirs, states that the attack was carried out by 300 Germans equipped with 81 mm mortars and other heavy weapons and that Renzo's unit, with only twenty or so elements, resisted for nine hours, but eventually had to retreat to Cigliè after being almost surrounded.

At the beginning of July, Mauri formed the 1st Sector Cuneo and Langhe, consisting of four large sectors:

- Alpine sector with almost 500 men divided between the Tanaro and Pesio valleys
- Alte Langhe sector with 12 detachments of 620 men deployed between the Colle di Montezemolo and Narzole
- Braidese sector with 150 men divided into two detachments
- Albese sector consisting of two detachments with a total of 110 men

Also at the disposal of the entire sector were the 'Muscun' Autonomous Guastatori Department under Lieutenant Renato Noè and a number of plain teams stationed between Cherasco, Narzole and Benevaglienna.

The men in Mauri's charge, however, continued to grow and by the end of the month, the 1st Sector Cuneo and Langhe was reorganised into three divisions, three brigades and several independent units:

- I 'Alpi' Division under the orders of Piero Cosa deployed in the Peveragno, Pesio, Ellero, Miroglio and Corsaglia valleys
- II 'Alps' Division commanded by Lieutenant Colonel Pier Alessandro Vanin deployed between the Casotto, Mongia and Tanaro valleys
- 'Langhe' Division under the orders of Mario Bogliolo deployed in the old Alte Langhe Sector
- 'Bra' Brigade under the command of Captain Icilio Ronchi Della Rocca deployed near the town of the same name
- 'Alba' Brigade commanded by Second Lieutenant Renato Carenzi and deployed near Alba
- 'Amendola' Brigade commanded by Colonel Roberto Ferrero, which grouped together the previously listed lowland units
- Detachment 'Marco' deployed in Sommariva Perno
- 'Franco' Detachment in Canale
- 'Carletto' detachment in Mango d'Alba
- Autonomous Guastatorial Department 'Muscun'

After a short time it changed its name to 1st Alpine Division Group.

From the end of July, the area between Bra, Murazzano, Carrù and Alba was affected by a combing carried out by two battalions of the Grenadier-Regiment 80. of the 34. Infanterie-Division supported by the Italian SS, C.A.R.S. forces and the I Mobile Brigade 'Vittorio Ricciarelli'.

---
24 Lorenzo Cesale, born in 1920, former lieutenant in the 8th Alpine Regiment.

During this raking, the 'Bra' Brigade was hit in the Pocapaglia area, forcing it to retreat to Ghigliani, in the 'Langhe' Division sector.

But the enemy action was extensive and also spread towards the Langhe; Mauri immediately organised himself to respond to the enemy action and sent two detachments to Dogliani, as well as undermining the carriageway between the village and Murazzano.

On 1 August, Bataillon 2 of Grenadier-Regiment 80. attacked the partisan positions at Dogliani and Belvedere, also occupying Murazzano, and forcing Mauri's forces to retreat to the strongholds of Marsaglia, Roccacigliè and Castellino.

The worst news was the capture of Mauri *by* some Germans while he was controlling the first line at Belvedere, and so the command passed to Bogliolo, who, in order not to create havoc, continued to issue orders signing himself Mauri.

The next day, the German attack continued, but the resistance of the 'Castellino' and 'Pedaggera' brigades managed to stem the enemy advance.

In the two days of fighting, the partisans had 6 dead and 19 wounded, while they claimed the killing of at least 75 Germans, a number that was certainly greatly inflated.

Regarding Mauri's capture in his memoirs, the Major states that he was transferred and treated in Cuneo, and then loaded into a car together with three Germans with destination Turin. During the journey the car was forced to stop because of a flat tyre and Mauri, still pretending to be in poor health, convinced one of the Germans to accompany him to the side of the road for a physiological need. In an instant, the Major escaped with all his strength, managing to join his men by 4 August.

In the text by Carlo Gentile, "I servizi segreti tedeschi in Italia 1943-1945", instead, a document is quoted, *BAB R 70 Italien/3*, which states: "*The ringleader Mauri [was] arrested [and is at the SD command] in Cuneo. Wiesner [sic] currently in Cuneo for negotiations [...] Mauri returns [to his partisan formations]. Agreement: no attacks against the Wm [i.e. the Wehrmacht]; information on communist groups; combing and garrisoning communist areas; first the communists and then Mauri*[25]".

Mauri, most probably, was released after an agreement made with Captain Adolf Wiessner, who had specially come from Verona to talk to the Major and failed to escape.

On 8 August, Mauri met with the commanders of the I and II 'Giustizia e Libertà' Division at Certosa di Pesio and an agreement was reached that included the two divisions, as well as all Jellist units in the province of Cuneo, under Mauri's command.

The 1st Alpine Division Group thus changed its name to 1st Alpine Division Group 'Justice and Freedom'.

Mauri's units also changed their names, the I and II 'Alps' Division were transformed into the III and IV Alpine G.L. Division, as were the two 'Langhe' divisions, which became the I and II 'Langhe' Division.

Even if the motto of 'Justice and Freedom' was adopted, the autonomous units under Mauri would have no interference from the Partito d'Azione and would remain strongly apolitical.

---

25 Text in German:" *Bandenführer Mauri festgenommen bei SD Cuneo. Wiesner z.Zt. in Cuneo [...] betr. Verhandlungen [...] Mauri zurück. Regelung: keine Angriffe auf Wm. Hinweise auf Kommunengruppen [sic]. Bekämpfung u. Nachsicherung von K[ommunistische]P[artei]-Räumen; erst K[ommunistische]P[artei], dann Mauri*". Taken from "I servizi segreti tedeschi in Italia 1943-1945", op. cit. in bibliography.

The agreement was short-lived and already on 4 September the pacts with the Jellists were cancelled.

On 16 August, another round-up began in the Langhe; one column, formed by the 1st Battalion of the 1st Regiment 'Hunters of the Apennines' and elements of the 1st Black Brigade 'Ather Capelli' - with the cooperation of the 'Bardelli' Company of the 'Ettore Muti' Legion - was to comb the area between Cherasco and Verduno, while a second column, with the 2nd Battalion of the 'Cacciatori degli Appennini' and a battalion of the I Mobile Black Brigade was to dislodge partisans located in Mango. The action was to be supported by a 47/32 gun section and two 20 mm sections of the Italian SS Kampfgruppe 'Heldman'.

The column advancing towards Mango was attacked on 16 August by elements of the Mango Detachment of the 'Belbo' Brigade near Torretta San Donato, causing the death of 15 soldiers of the 2nd Battalion (partisan sources speak of 36 dead and 50 wounded), while the autonomous men lost 11 men.

On the 17th, a column of Italian SS trucks was attacked on the road between Pollenzo and Santa Vittorie d'Alba with the loss of a truck.

The round-up ended on the 20th with minimal results, because the partisans retreated without engaging in much fighting.

The last round of raids started on 29 August, targeting the area between Pollenzo and Narzole. 400 men from the two 'Hunters of the Apennines' regiments, a hundred men of the 1st Mobile Black Brigade, four companies of the Ost-Bataillon 617. and a 47/32 cannon section of Kampfgruppe 'Heldman'[26] were mobilised for the action.

The action started in the early morning of the 29th, deploying two columns, one heading towards Alba and the other towards Monforte d'Alba, clashing with the 'Bra' Brigade and the 48ª Garibaldi Brigade, who, however, managed to disengage from the fight, limiting their losses.

The action ended on 2 September. According to partisan sources, the Italo-Germans had 30 dead and 50 wounded, while the partisans lost two men.

Republican sources declared one dead and two wounded among the ranks of the 2nd Regiment 'Hunters of the Apennines' and two wounded among the German troops.

The forces at Mauri's disposal increased more and more and by September 1944 he had 5,600 men under his orders, divided as follows:

- I 'Langhe' Division under the command of Mario Bogliolo in four brigades (Castellino, Langhe Ovest, Pedaggera and Mondovì)
- II 'Langhe' Division under the orders of Piero Balbo 'Poli' in three brigades (Belbo, Canale and Asti)
- III 'Alps' Division under the command of Piero Cosa in three brigades (Val Pesio, Val Ellero and Val Corsaglia)
- IV 'Alpi' Division under the command of Lieutenant Colonel Alessandro Vanni in three brigades (Val Casotto, Val Mongia and Val Tanaro).
- Three autonomous brigades: Alba, Brà and Amendola

---

26 The book 'Feeling - Thinking - Wanting History of the Italian SS Legion' also states of the use of elements from the 'Monte Rosa' Division, the X MAS and the 'Leonessa' Armoured Group, op. cit. in bibliography.

After the occupation of Alba at the beginning of October and the subsequent reconquest by the Republicans, the entire resistance system of the Langhe was involved in a very harsh round-up that hit the 1st Alpine Division Group very hard.

It was not until the beginning of January that Mauri's forces recovered with a total of 3,280 men divided into five divisions and two brigades, which continued to carry out various disruptive actions against the Republican and German forces.

As the general uprising approached, the units of the 1st Alpine Division Group increased, as did the numerous actions against the enemy and also the raids suffered. On 3 March, Operation Marder was launched against the positions of the 1st 'Langhe' Division between Castellino Tanaro and Clavesana; the attack was carried out by elements of the Grenadier-Regiment 80., the 1st Battalion 'Granatieri di Sardegna' of the 'Cacciatori degli Appennini' Regiment and elements of the Republican National Guard.

The action forced the partisans to retreat, leaving 15 dead on the ground (according to Axis sources 30) while the Italo-Germans had 5 dead and 10 wounded - partisan sources exaggerate the number to 70 dead and 150 wounded -[27].

But by then the situation for the Axis forces was irreparable and on the eve of the general uprising, the 1st Alpine Division Group was structured as follows:

- I 'Langhe' Division under the command of Mario Bogliolo in seven brigades (1st Castellino, 2nd Mondovì, 3rd Langhe Ovest, 4th Pedaggera, lst Valle Bormida and 2nd)
- II 'Langhe' Division under the orders of Piero Balbo 'Poli' in four brigades (5th Belbo, 6th Valle Uzzone, 7th Rocca d'Arazzo and 8th Grana)
- IV 'Alps' Division under the orders of Ferdinando Travaglio 'Peschiera' in three brigades (13th Val Tanaro, 14th Mongia Valley and 15th Val Casotto)
- V 'Monferrato' Division commanded by Giuseppe Cravera in three brigades (17th Asti, 18th and 19th)
- VI 'Asti' Division under the orders of Giovanni Toselli 'Otello' in three brigades (21st San Damiano, 22nd Alba and 25th Canale)
- XII 'Bra' Division under the command of Captain Icilio Ronchi Della Rocca in four brigades (45th, 46th, 47th and 48th)
- XV 'Alessandria' Division under the orders of Stefano Cigliano 'Mimmo' in two brigades (57th and 58th)
- 103rd 'Amendola' Brigade commanded by Renato Gancia 'Rabbia'

With the beginning of the insurrection, Mauri gave different objectives to his units; the 21st 'San Damiano' and 25th 'Canale' Brigades of the VI 'Asti' Division were sent towards Turin, as was the 5th 'Belbo' Brigade of the II 'Langhe' Division, which was to head towards the Piedmontese capital after occupying Alba.

The I 'Langhe' Division instead liberated - together with other partisan units - Mondovì, Fossano, Savigliano, Racconigi and Cavallermaggiore.

The other units of the 1st Alpine Division Group contributed to the liberation of other locations in Piemont.

---

[27] Taken from Renzo Amedeo, "Diario Mauri. Marzo 1945" and Leonardo Sandri, "Il Raggruppamento 'Cacciatori degli Appennini'. Una documentazione", op. cit. in bibliography

Garibaldi Departments

In May 1944, the 1st Garibaldi 'Piedmont' Division, operating in the western part of the province of Cuneo, set up two brigades in the Langhe: the 16th 'General Perotti'[28], a former detachment of the 4th Brigade, and the 48th 'Dante di Nanni' formed with partisans recruited between Cuneo and Alba.

In August 1944, by joining these two brigades and the 78th 'Red Star' Brigade[29] of Giovanni Rocca Primo[30] the VI Garibaldi Division 'Langhe' was formed under the orders of Giovanni Latilla.

At the beginning of September, the Garibaldians of the VI Division occupied various towns in the Langhe such as Serralunga, La Morra, Castiglion Falletto, Barolo, Dogliani, Bossolasco, S. Benedetto, Cravanzana, Niella, Belbo and Mombarcaro while the divisional command was based in Monforte. In September, the 48th Brigade in particular was very active in the Alba area. Towards the end of the month, it employed a detachment almost every day to carry out night actions in the town of Alba.

These actions caused the Axis forces to react and on 1 October they attacked the positions of the 16th Brigade deployed between the Bormida Valley and the Belbo Valley.

At the end of 1944, with the increase in the numbers, the Raggruppamento Divisioni d'Assalto Garibaldi delle Langhe (Garibaldi Assault Divisions Grouping of the Langhe) was formed, which had the VI Garibaldi Division 'Langhe' and the VIII Garibaldi Division 'Asti' (operating in the Asti area with the 45th 'Ateo Garemi' brigades, 78th 'Devic' and 98th 'Martyrs of Alessandria'[31]) and the IX Garibaldi Division 'Alarico Imerito' (formed in November in Monferrato with the 78th 'Devic', 101st 'Bona' and 102nd 'Sulic' brigades).

In January, the 14th Garibaldi Division 'Luigi Capriolo' was formed (formed by the 48th 'Dante di Nanni' Brigade, the 179th 'Carlo Lamberti' Brigade and the 180th 'Marco Conterno' Brigade), while the 6th Division remained with only two brigades: the 16th 'Generale Perotti' and the 99th 'Luigi Fiore' Brigade, while the Islafran Detachment was transformed into the Divisional Arditi Group under the 212th 'Giuseppe Maruffi' Brigade.

Shortly afterwards, the 103rd 'Nannetti' Brigade was formed between Val San Lorenzo and Ceresole d'Alba.

From February, the Garibaldini were very active, even hitting two roadblocks in the city of Alba at Porta Savona and Via Piave on the night of 15[32].

In March, the actions increased and on the 20th the 48th Garibaldi Brigade 'Dante di Nanni', together with the 12th Autonomous Division 'Bra', occupied Cherasco, leading to the reaction of the Republicans who already on the 25th attacked the positions of the 99th Garibaldi Brigade 'Luigi Fiore' between Murazzano and Dogliani; the unit was supported by the action of the 16th Garibaldi Brigade 'Generale Perotti' and the attack repulsed.

---

28 With commander Giovanni Latilla 'Nanni' and deputy commander Luigi Fiore
29 It later changed its name to 'Devic', dedicated to Angelo Prete 'Devic', commander of the 16th Garibaldi Brigade 'Generale Perotti' from August 1944, killed by a Garibaldi partisan - Il Biondino - on 31 August 1944 in Cortemilia. The partisan in question then went on to join the ranks of Mauri's Autonomists.
30 Former soldier of the 29th Infantry Regiment 'Assietta' class of 1921
31 In the text 'Storia Partigiana della Divisione Autonoma XV Alessandria', op. cit. in bibliography, Stefano Cigliano 'Mimmo', commander first of the VIII Garibaldi Division and then of the XV 'Alessandria', states that the division's staff was made up of 45th, 98th and 100th Garibaldi Brigade.
32 The action was carried out by the Jules Detachment of the 48th Garibaldi Brigade 'Dante di Nanni'.

In April, the actions towards Alba continued, culminating in two actions, namely the fight between Sommariva and Ceresole d'Alba, carried out by the 103rd Garibaldi Brigade 'Nannetti', the 45th Autonomous Brigade of the XII Autonomous Division 'Bra' and elements of the III 'Justice and Freedom' Division, and the attack on Alba on 15 April.

Immediately afterwards, the Garibaldini occupied Cherasco again on 19 while the 180th Garibaldi Brigade 'Marco Conterno' attacked the Republican garrisons of Dogliani and Murazzano and forced them to surrender in the following days.

With the outbreak of the General Insurrection, the Garibaldi forces of the Garibaldi Assault Divisions Grouping of the Langhe were sent towards Turin to contribute, together with other units, to the liberation of the Piedmontese capital.

G.L. Departments

In the spring of 1944, the first 'Giustizia e Libertà' band was born in the Alba area, the 7th Banda G.L. under the orders of Captain Giovanni Alessandria, which initially operated with the support of the Jellist units stationed in the western Cuneo area. In August, the death of Captain Alessandria and the capture of the deputy commander - Lieutenant Piero Mancuso - led the small band to place itself under Mauri's forces, remaining dislocated near Murazzano under the orders of Lieutenant Libero Porcari and then breaking away from the Autonomists after the break of the agreements and settling between Neive and Castagnole Lanze.

The first real Jellist forces arrived in the Langhe only in December 1944 with the dispatch of some groups from the 2nd G.L. Division, stationed in Val Maira and Val Varaita. The new groups joined the 7th G.L. Band, settling in January between Neive, Neviglie, Mango, Castagnole and Castiglione d'Asti.

With these units the III G.L. Division 'Langhe' was created with commander Alberto Bianco, but some internal problems led to a break-up of the unit and the birth in mid-February of the X G.L. Division 'Langhe' with commander Giorgio Bocca and formed by three brigades initially stationed between Neviglie and Mango.

The two units continued to have disputes due to the decision of the G.L. Regional Command to return some units of the X G.L. Division to the III; the X commands managed to avoid the transfers with the exception of a brigade stationed in Val Bormida, which was handed over entirely to the III G.L. Division.

In any case, the two units were two small divisions of 500 to 700 men.

On 13 March, there was a change of command within the X G.L. Division that saw the appointment of Raimondo Paglieri as commander while Giorgio Bocca was transferred to the II G.L. Division as political commissar.

Relations with the other partisan units stationed in the Langhe were good, especially those with the Garibaldini, who saw the G.L. as a good hook against the overwhelming power of Mauri's autonomous forces, as well as being very useful because they often handed over their weapons to the Allies.

Towards March, the two divisions were united and became part of the 1st Group of G.L. Divisions of the Cuneo area and in April the G.L. forces took part in the aforementioned clash between Sommariva and Ceresole d'Alba as well as the attack on Alba on the 15th.

At the outbreak of the General Insurrection, the III G.L. Division advanced towards Turin while the X G.L. Division on Asti.

Matteotti Departments

In the summer of 1944, a small group of twenty ex-autonomists under the command of Paolo Farinetti made contact with the Socialist Party and settled in the Langhe - between Barbaresco, Treiso, Trezzo and Neive - and Monferrato.

At the beginning of January 1945, from this group the 21st Matteotti Brigade 'Fratelli Ambrogio' was formed, which operated in close collaboration with the Mauri Autonomists and took part in the liberation of Alba in cooperation with the II 'Langhe' Division.

▲ Militiamen of the Republican National Guard leaving for an action on board a FIAT 626 truck. The G.N.R. garrison in Turin took an active part in the operations in Alba in November 1944 (Cucut).

▲ The centre of Alba seen from the heights surrounding the town: from the image it is clear how important it was for any attacker (both partisans and republicans) to have control of the hills in order to carry out an effective firing manoeuvre on the town.

▼ Soldiers of the Autonomous Cavalry Squadron of the Army General Staff with the unit's flag; on the cap can be seen the canutilla frieze, formed by a grenade with a straight flame. A Platoon from Bergamo under the command of Captain Bussotti took part in the fighting at Alba (Arena).

▲ Close-up of a Cavalry Cavalry Squadron of the Anti-Partisan Regiment (Arena).

▼ Anti-Partisan Regiment patrol in the Langhe (Arena).

▲ The very young Cavalryman Giuseppe Giaroni, portrayed at the beginning of 1944 in Bergamo, where the Autonomous Cavalry Squadron of the Army General Staff was being formed. He still wears the stars on his jacket and has the frieze of the 'Savoia Cavalry' Regiment, from which he came (Giaroni).

▲ Another studio photograph of Cavaliere Carlo Giaroni: on his jacket the white three-pointed flames with the gladius of the Cavalry of the National Republican Army. In the original photo, the tie was hand-dyed red (Giaroni).

▲ Group of Knights from the Autonomous Cavalry Squadron of the Army General Staff in training in Bergamo (Giaroni).

▲ Carlo Giaroni in Bergamo (Giaroni).

▲ A group of officers and soldiers of the Autonomous Cavalry Unit of the Anti-Partisan Regiment: the photograph shows the use of the three-pointed white flames and the countershoulders, also threaded in white, on the uniforms of the pre-armist model (Giaroni).

▼ Some of the soldiers of the Autonomous Cavalry Department, portrayed in the previous photograph, show their skills on horseback (Giaroni).

▲ Autonomous Cavalry Patrol of the Anti-Partisan Regiment on the heights around Alba (Giaroni).

▲ Another image of the same patrol: the horseman holding the reins is a veteran of the 'Savoia Cavalry' who fought in Russia, as he has the pinned to the breast of his jacket (Giaroni).

▲ Knights of the Anti-Partisan Regiment in Alba, probably in the last days of the war (Giaroni).

▲ A platoon of men from the R.A.P. Cavalry Squadron in Turin on 23 March 1945, on the occasion of the impressive demonstration held for the 28th anniversary of the founding of the Fasci di Combattimento (Pisanò).

▼ Military operations during the civil war in the Republic of Alba and the Free Zone of Monferrato (summer-autumn 1944) (Emanuele Mastrangelo - CC BY-SA 3.0).

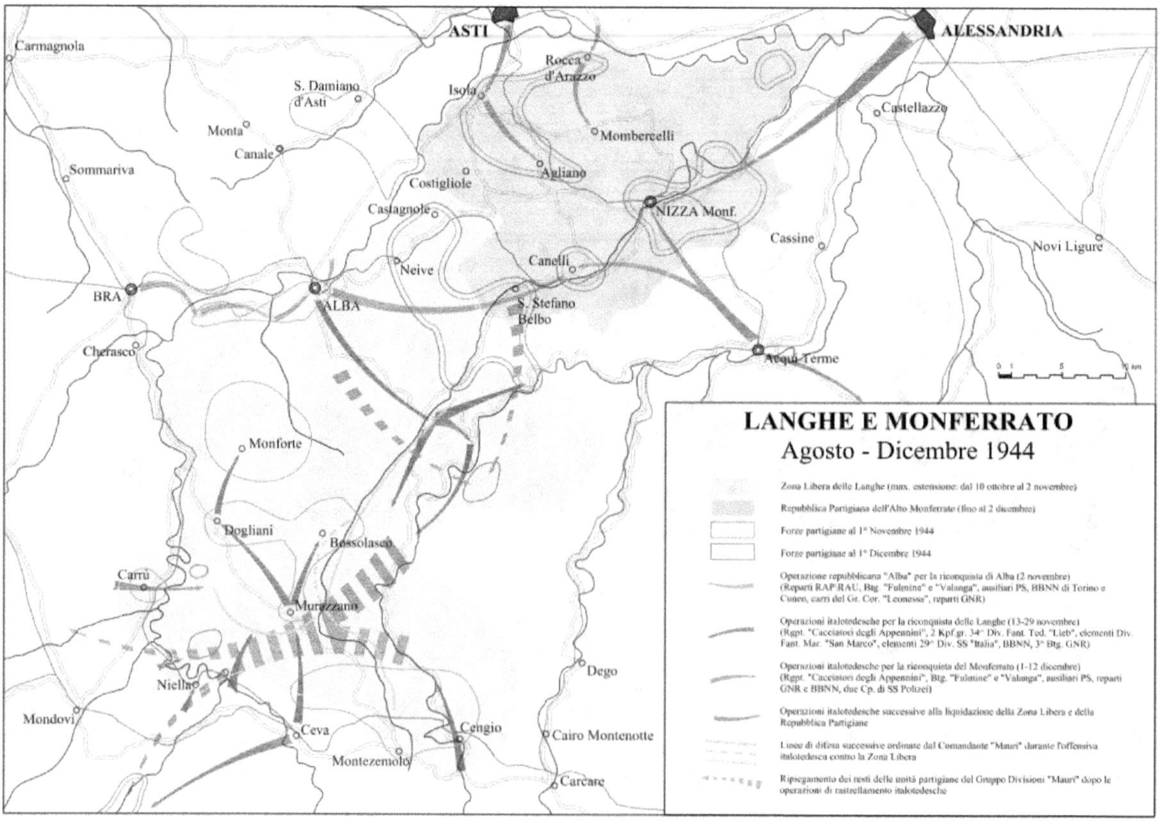

▲ Two Armed Forces officers on board a Lancia Aprilia in the King's outfit, probably of civilian origin (Gallesi).

▼ Officers of the Anti-Partisan Regiment in the Bra area in April 1945 (Cucut).

▲ Partisans of the 2nd 'Langhe' Division in front of the Church of the Battuti di Mango in February 1945 (WEB source).

▼ Partisan Armando Meniciatti and brothers Giuliano and Walden Cirelli, members of the 3rd Justice and Freedom Division, escorted by two soldiers of the 'Cacciatori degli Appennini' (Apennine Hunters), in anticipation of their execution in Monchiero d'Alba on 9 March 1945 (Crippa).

▲ Brothers Giuliano and Walden Cirelli of the 3rd Justice and Freedom Division 'Langhe' before being shot at Monchiero d'Alba on 9 March 1945 ('Resistenza - Album della Guerra di Liberazione').

▼ Four partisans of the 21st Matteotti Brigade 'Fratelli Ambrogio' on a truck armed with a Breda 30 machine gun and a Maschinengewehr 34 ('Gazzetta d'Alba').

▲ Giorgio Bocca (centre), commander of the 10th Justice and Freedom Division and later commissioner of the 2nd G.L. Division, with other Jellist partisans probably in a photo taken at the beginning of the resistance experience ('Patria Indipendente').

▼ Partisans of the 'Islafran' Detachment of the 48th 'Dante di Nanni' Brigade in a group photograph (WEB source).

▲ Soldiers of the Canuck mission fire a 3-inch mortar at Republican positions in Alba during the attack on 15 April 1945 (from 'Excelsior - The Partisan Airport').

▼ Two partisans on the heights of Alba probably during the attack on 15 April 1945. Note the use of a spyglass and a Bren machine gun ('Alba for Freedom').

▲ Partisans of the 48th 'Garibaldi' Brigade.

▼ Three Canadian soldiers from the Canuck mission of the 2nd SAS, which arrived at Mauri's units in April 1945, armed with a water-cooled Vickers machine gun near the village of Castino (WEB source).

R.S.I. UNITS GARRISONED IN ALBA FROM SUMMER 1944 TO MAY 1945

On the Republican side, the town of Alba was garrisoned by a variable contingent of military units during the period examined in this text. What is striking, however, is how, starting from the 'reconquest' of the town in November 1944, a rather substantial garrison was set up, proving the strategic importance of the Langhe town, so much so that an Artillery Battery was deployed continuously.

The units all belonged to the Anti-Partisan Regiment; this unit arose from the summer of 1944, as the second Co.Gu. (Counter Guerrilla) light brigade in support of the 'Hunters of the Apennines' Regiment, to be used in the fight against the partisans. The Anti-Partisan Regiment consisted of:

- Group Headquarters
- 4 Armed Forces Battalions:
    - I Battalion Arditi Bersaglieri
    - II Battalion Arditi Fanti
    - III Alpine Armed Forces Battalion
    - IV Battalion Arditi Fanti
- I Autonomous Cavalry Department
- X Special Artillery Group
- Light Wagon Company
- Mixed Genie Company
- 2 Reparti Arditi Ufficiali (R.A.U.):
    - 1ST R.A.U.
    - 2ND R.A.U.
- Team X (espionage and infiltration unit).

Under the command of Colonel Alessandro Ruta, the R.A.P. was deployed in Turin and Piedmont with anti-partisan tasks and was in arms until early May 1945. Some units surrendered to the Americans and were taken to concentration camps, others had worse luck, like the 2nd R.A.U., whose elements were slaughtered[33].

The evolution of the staffing of the republican military garrison in Alba can be summarised by analysing its constitution at three fundamental moments: up to October 1944 (thus until the seizure by the partisans), from November 1944 (after the 'reconquest' by the Social Republic) and in April 1945, the last phase of the war.

October 1944:

- II Cadore Battalion of the 'Hunters of the Apennines' Regiment
- a garrison of the Republican National Guard (probably formed by personnel from the 3rd G.N.R. Battalion of the 'Hunters of the Apennines' Regiment)

---

[33] For more on the history of the Regiment, see 'I reparti controguerriglia della R.S.I.' by Paolo Crippa and Carlo Cucut, work cited in the bibliography.

From November 1944 (after the reoccupation of the city):
- II Infantrymen Battalion of the Anti-Partisan Regiment
- 1 Cavalry Squadron Platoon of the Anti-Partisan Regiment
- 1 Battery 75/13 of the X Special Artillery Group of the Anti-Partisan Regiment

April 1945:
- II Infantrymen Battalion of the Anti-Partisan Regiment
- III Alpine Armed Forces Battalion of the Anti-Partisan Regiment (from 15 April 1945)
- 1 Cavalry Squadron Platoon of the Anti-Partisan Regiment
- 1 Battery 75/13 of the X Special Artillery Group of the Anti-Partisan Regiment
- 1 Platoon of the 1 Light Tank Company (on 4 L3 wagons) of the Anti-Partisan Regiment (in town since January 1945)

II Battalion Arditi Fanti

The constitution of the Arditi Battalions to be included in the Anti-Partisan Regiment dates back to July 1944, when it was planned to create three Battalions to be trained specifically for counter-guerrilla warfare, about 2,000 strong. Between July and November, these units were actually formed; in fact, one more was formed than planned.

The II Battaglione Arditi Fanti, born as II Battaglione Controguerriglia and also known as Battaglione 'Tito Speri', had a long gestation period. In fact, it began in August 1944 in Brescia, but was not completed until November, when it was in Piedmont. It was articulated on:

- 2nd Commando Platoon - commander Second Lieutenant Benito Caramanti
- 3 Rifle Companies:
    - 5th Rifle Company - Commander: Captain Hamlet Rossi
    - 6th Rifle Company
    - 7th Rifle Company
- 8th Accompanying Arms Company - commander: Captain Arturo Cingano

The Battalion saw Lieutenant Colonel Pieroni, Lieutenant Colonel Palomba and Major Gagliardo Gagliardi succeed each other in command. It was based in Turin, with a Platoon stationed in Alba and one in Cherasco; after the reoccupation of Alba in November 1944, almost the entirety of the Battalion (Headquarters, 5th Rifle Company and 8th Heavy Weapons Company) was placed to garrison the city until the end of the war.

During the partisan attack in Alba on 15 April 1945, the Battalion was stationed at various points in the city. The Commando Platoon was stationed in the Minor Seminary and played a non-frontline role during the fighting, as is also stated in Lieutenant Caramanti's report: "On the *morning of the 15th, as the partisan attack was looming, the men in the reserve de-*

ployed to defend the posts previously assigned by the Battalion Commander. The three men serving at the Telephone Exchange, half an hour before the attack, realised that a time bomb had been placed in front of the main door. They immediately went out with their weapons and, having gone about 20 metres away from the telephone exchange, Capt. Maj. Montelatici fired a musket shot at the bomb, causing it to explode, a burst that alarmed the Presidium. Then the three men fell back, one to the 8th Company's base and two to the Command Platoon headquarters.

At 10 am, the Platoon was commanded to escort Lt. Medic Colucci who was on his way to medicate the wounded of the 8th Comp. A.A. On the way he was fired upon by automatic weapons, which were answered with a few bursts of machine gun fire, proceeding towards the 8th Company which was reached without any casualties. While the doctor treated the wounded, the men, as far as possible, joined those of the 8th Company. to fire on partisan elements that had infiltrated the Seminary and were pounding the defence positions of that compound with various automatic weapons.

Meanwhile, the daring Bruno joined a squad from the 5th Comp. which went to the Caserma Govone to look for the radio fitter who lived in Piazza Savona to come and repair the radio transmitter that had been stationary for two hours. The squad at Porta Savona was attacked by strong partisan nuclei; despite this Bruno threw himself into the fray, but was shot in the chest and left leg, forcing him and the squad to barricade themselves in a house. Corporal Soldi also distinguished himself with this squad.

At 11.30 a.m. the Commando Platoon returned to the barracks without losses. In the afternoon, elements of the Platoon competed to bring orders to the 8th A.A. Company and the Govone Barracks. Particularly distinguished was the daring Santucci, who went out seven times alone, always returning to his headquarters. Capt. Maj. Magliocco joined Lt. Moltrer to raid the Seminary area. During the night, the Platoon went out twice more to transport mortars and ammunition from 8th Company to 5th Company. Once the arms transport was finished, six men were ordered to reinforce the 8th Comp. A.A.

Throughout the action, the department suffered the following losses:

Missing men: S. Lt. Bernardini Settimio (who went out on ambush the night before and did not return)[34]; wounded: ardito Bruno Giovanni'.

It is interesting to note that, with great immodesty, Second Lieutenant Benito Caramanti nominated as many as 12 of his subordinates for promotions, medals for valour and war crosses, despite the marginal contribution made to the fighting by the Platoon Command. None of them, however, appeared on the list of field decorations drawn up by General Archimede Mischi.

Commanded by Captain Amleto Rossi, the 5th Company was, unlike the Platoon Command, the unit most exposed to the fury of the battle. The unit was stationed near the Minor Seminary and was also in charge of the garrison at Porta Vivaro and Porta Savona, where the most violent phases of the partisan attack took place on 15 April. Below is the central part of Captain Rossi's report, which describes in detail the clashes sustained by his Company:

"[...] At 6.12 a.m. the enemy began the attack with a raging fire of artillery and light and

---

[34] It is unclear whether the officer was captured or killed by partisans or whether he deserted voluntarily.

heavy automatic weapons. The enemy initially placed the greatest effort of the attack in the Tanaro sector, an effort that was immediately contained due to the precise and calm reaction of the defence sector assigned to that side and commanded by Te. Moltrer Mario. After about half an hour of fire, the pressure of the Tanaro sector could be considered crushed by the losses visible in corpses on the riverbank and the enemy retreated its line, giving the Porta Tanaro blockade post the opportunity to fall back. From this moment on, however, the volume of fire from the Angeli hill, the bridge over the Cherasca and the bell tower, the highest point of the city, increased.

Fire from the latter centres pounded the courtyard of the barracks, making it difficult for the artillery pieces to manoeuvre and for the tanks to enter and exit. At about 7 a.m., the outlaws began shelling the barracks with British grenade launchers, British '55 mortars and '47 cannons. The shells caused damage to the building, unhinged doors and windows and demolished the protective walls.

I ordered the Brixia mortars of '45 to go into action to hit some of the grenade-throwing positions, especially the positions to the right of the Cherasca protected by the mill building. The enemy grenade-throwing positions on the Cherasca fell silent and, on the other hand, grenades began to arrive from the north of the town, which in the meantime had been occupied by the rebels.

At 10:30 a.m., I sent out a squad under the command of Lt. Marquez to engage the rebel forces that had entered the city in order to be able to keep the College - Boarding School and Minor Seminary area, respective 8th and 5th Company camps, clear.

At 11.30 a.m. I came out of the barracks realising the situation that at that moment, after six hours of fighting, could be presented as follows: the whole town, with the exception of the Convitto - Minor Seminary blocks were in the hands of the outlaws. A squad barricaded in a house on Via Mazzini and bravely fighting by resisting intimidation to surrender constituted another of our centres of fire.

All the roadblocks, with the exception of Porta Cherasca bravely defended by the Knights of the Autonomous Cavalry Squadron, were overwhelmed and had fallen back.

The rebel forces occupied the settlements overlooking the barracks, holding it under fire from automatic weapons and grenade launchers.

At about 12.30 p.m., by relay, I learnt of the critical situation of the 8th A.A. Company, forced into the short space of the entrance hall, to have the courtyard and the dormitories beaten by direct fire from grenade launchers and heavy automatic weapons. I sent in reinforcement and with the task of occupying the Bishop's Palace, attacking it from behind, a platoon of Lt. Moltrer Mario who razed part of the Vescovado, flushing out the nearest rebel forces that were beating the nucleus of the 8th A.A. Company from 20 metres), thus giving the possibility of partially rebuilding a defence nucleus and recovering the mortars that had to be abandoned in the courtyard.

At 15.30, due to the pressing request for help from the 8th A.A. Company located at the Collegio Convitto base, I once again sent a platoon under the command of Lt. Moltrer Mario who, while attempting to outflank a building in which 15 outlaws with automatic weapons were barricaded, was hit by a grenade, dying instantly, together with the daring bersagliere Mezzetti Giacomo, a cook, who had volunteered to help.

Towards 6pm, enemy pressure slowed to a crawl, and the barricaded forces could be brought

together and the besieged nuclei returned to their camps.
Losses sustained by the Company: dead no. 2; injured no. 3; missing no. 12.
The night found the men still awake at their posts, ready to resume the fight and the approaching movement of partisan forces evidently still attempting the attack. In the middle of the night the partisan forces moved away from the area, presumably informed by relay girls of the approaching column of reinforcements'.

The Porta Savona checkpoint, as we have seen, had turned out to be one of the focal points of the partisan attack, resisting doggedly for over five hours, and its fall seemed to be the prelude to victory for the partisans, who, however, were unable to complete their capture of the city. The resistance put up by the fascists was so fierce that the episode had the honour of being mentioned in the Order of the Day of 18 April 1945 in paragraph 313, which we quote below because, although steeped in rhetoric, the treatment of the facts is adherent to reality and well detailed:

"HEROIC RESISTANCE AT ONE OF OUR CHECKPOINTS:
From the testimony of burghers relating to the defence of the Porta Savona checkpoint in the attack of 15.4.45 - burghers who acted as intermediaries between our soldiers and the partisans - we have learned the following: - At 6.60 a.m. the attack on the Porta Savona checkpoint began at close range. Six shots from grenade launchers dismantled the main defences of the checkpoint from the first minutes. The enemy, supported by Bren fire from both the avenue of Moretta and the railway gully managed to surround the blockade.

Three intimations of surrender were sent to our men: the replies were machine-gun fire. The rebels, seeing the futility of their efforts, sent two burghers to bargain; S.Lt. Pierani Giovanni - commander of the blockade post - wounded in the groin, both thighs and one arm, continued to incite the men and refused to surrender. When urged by some of the villagers to desist from the unequal fight, the officer replied that he was a man of honour and would not surrender until he had ammunition.

The partisans blew up the gate with plastic mines and threw themselves down the stairs: one was stabbed by one of our daring men, another riddled with bullets; the enemy fell back with several wounded. The fire flared up again; S.Lt. Pierani accepted that the civilians evacuated from the blockhouse and with his men helped them to safety. Further intimations to surrender were made with the threat that the blockhouse would be blown up with dynamite; the response was always negative.

S.Lt. Pierani, no longer able to lead the men due to physical impossibility, gave the direction of the stronghold to Capt. Magni.

At 11.45 a.m. - after more than five hours of resistance - a gang leader, a certain Mario, sent two civilians to parliament; Lieutenant Pierani, who was left with four magazines, declared that he would only speak on the condition that the partisan presented himself to him unarmed, which he accepted, presenting himself in a stiff salute and praising all the soldiers who had honourably resisted twelve against more than two hundred.

The commander of the checkpoint asked:
honour of arms for all men;
1. *intangibility of people;*
2. *continue to wear the uniform of the Republican Army;*

3. remain united in the concentration camp;
4. adequate nourishment of the men themselves.

Having accepted these conditions from both sides, Lieutenant Pierani emerged from the checkpoint at the head of his men, armed and in perfect order, and marched in front of the enemy to the corner of Via S. Paolo, at which point the men laid down their weapons, while the officer kept his pistol.

The partisan leader who had signed the surrender and the commander of the attack operation in Alba congratulated the officer and supported him on his wounds that prevented him from walking.

Arditi of the 2nd Battalion, it is with faith that the enemy is dismayed; even an outlaw bows reverently before the valour of a true soldier and in surrender recognises the honour of arms!"

Finally, the 8th Company was stationed at the city's Civic Boarding School, armed with 6 mortars and light and heavy machine guns, and also had a detachment guarding Porta Tanaro; during the course of the day, it had 4 dead and 11 wounded, including the commander Captain Cingano himself, who recounted the day's events in his report:

"On the morning of the 15th at approximately 6 a.m., the first explosion took place in Piazza del Duomo. Having made telephone contact with the roadblock and the Battalion Headquarters, at around 6.05 a.m., the second explosion occurred, interrupting telephone communications. I gave the alarm to the officers and troops who were already 'on the alert'.

I sent out three patrols:

(a) under the orders of S.Lt. Migliori to connect with the checkpoint
(b) Sgt. Ghedina to take orders from Battalion Headquarters
(c) of S.Lt. Forcisi to carry out a reconnaissance of the telephone exchange.

As per initial directives received by telephone, I have three mortar rounds fired towards Porta Tanaro. It was about 6.20 a.m. when the attack on the city began with extremely violent fire. I immediately start firing two mortars against the ridge facing Porta Cherasca (11 shots fired). In the meantime, the patrol of S.Lt. Ghedina's full patrol returns. After the third shot, a bomb remained inert in the firing tube; while the officer, assisted by Sgt. A.U. Cortese was preparing to remove the bomb, fire was opened from the windows of the Major Seminary towards the Barracks courtyard (about 6.35 a.m.). The officer and the non-commissioned officer were wounded in the first volley. At the same time, fire is opened from the Piazza del Duomo against the main entrance.

I am forced to make the servants of the six mortars placed in the courtyard fall back to safety. With the protection of the machine gun placed at the door, S.Lt. Migliori and four soldiers from the other two patrols.

...Inwards the duel from the windows begins...

Around 7 a.m. part of the team under the command of S.Lt. Saviano, who was on duty at the checkpoint. Missing are: the ard. Pedrali Giulio, carrying the tripod, shot dead in Piazza del Duomo, the two non-commissioned officers, Sgt. A.U. Carrino Norberto and Sgt. A.U. Martini Egidio, who will be found slaughtered in the evening, and Ard. Dotti Costantino, who had picked up the trunk abandoned by Pedrali and who, having been wounded in the legs, had had to surrender before the partisans who had emerged from Via Coppa (this partisan patrol was commanded by former 5th Company soldier Martini, a Mauritian officer, and also included former Arditi Mondini of the 5th Company and Ronconi of the 8th Company). A few metres from the barracks, the daring Benedetti was wounded in the back and was able to reach the entrance but had to abandon the machine gun he was carrying.

Around 8 o'clock, a new threat looms: the outlaws, having occupied the adjoining church, attempt to break into the cellar, breaking through the door to the room that has been converted into a kitchen. The danger can be dealt with by placing the machine gun removed from the front door for protection.

Protected by the machine-gun fire on the upper floor, I attempt the offensive against the Seminary with the grenade launcher: after three shots (two of which hit), as I am about to launch the fourth, I am wounded by the burst of the same bomb that I was about to launch (around 10 o'clock).

From this moment on, while not relinquishing command, Lt. Col. Mazzara and Lt. Piersanti. The duel continues with alternating threats, sometimes from the kitchen, sometimes from the main entrance. Around 11 o'clock, s.t.l. Forcisi and ard. Riboni wounded in the foot; both managed to escape capture by sheltering with civilians.

Around 1.3 p.m., as the situation was still critical, I sent Capt. Maj. Colombo and the daring Olivieri to the roof of the Chapel with the order to attempt the launch of 10 Sipe hand grenades on the roof of the Seminary. The two succeeded in the mission entrusted to them and there was a feeling of diminished pressure, so I gave the order to Lt. Migliori and S.Lt. Melosi to attempt the recovery of at least one mortar. Capt. Maj. Colombo volunteers to collaborate. The recovery succeeded, but at the cost of the heroic sacrifice of the corporal himself.

Around 4.15 p.m., the Arditi Valentino and Tumiatti return. Valentino informs me that he and his comrade had been captured by the partisans, that they had taken with them to the hospital because they were wounded, Maj. Vittorielli, that he found Ard. Dotti and having been released, as a former partisan, to come and take possession of the machine gun. A squad of 6 or 7 men, including Gallori (who escaped from Alba Prison) and Pregliasco (ex-Ardito of the 8th Comp.), with a bren and a grenade launcher, placed themselves at the level of the arcades in front of the Calissano bar, offending the door of the barracks and waiting for him to return with the machine gun. I immediately warn the guards not to let Lt. Mazzara and s.ten Melosi that with two men I had previously sent to the Btg. command to take orders and agreements and at the same time I let s.ten. Piersanti to beat the position in Piazza Duomo with a mortar.

Warned of the threat by the officer on guard, Lt. Moltrer orders his platoon to go around the position, but in that moment a grenade, possibly thrown at the barracks, falls almost at his feet, killing him together with Cpt. Mezzettetti of the 5th Platoon, who was at his side. Immediately afterwards comes a second grenade that falls a little to the left of the barracks door. I continue firing the mortar into Piazza del Duomo and the houses facing it and the desired effect is obtained: the enemy abandons the position (about 17.30 hours).

The first news of the partisans' departure from the town began to arrive; having eliminated the offence towards the courtyard, all the mortars were once again available and I therefore gave the order to fire a few shots - 18 - in the direction of Madonna degli Angeli, where movement was noted.

At around 7 p.m. the first civilians are noticed and I have confirmation that the outlaws have *abandoned the town. I consider the attack over and, after giving some directives for the night defence, I hand over command temporarily to Lt. Mezzara and s.ten. Piersanti.*

Still missing from the roll-call is Ard. Portesi, who went out on patrol in the morning, but returned the next day with all his weapons, having managed to escape capture by taking refuge in the boarding school of the Luigine Sisters.

Unfortunately, from all the soldiers killed or captured, the partisans removed their individual weapons. The losses sustained during the day are as follows: 2 non-commissioned officers killed; 1 NCO killed; 1 NCO wounded; 3 wounded soldiers; 2 soldiers captured but then released; all disarmed because they were shot outside the compound; 1 NCO dead; 2 officers wounded (including myself); 1 NCO wounded; 4 soldiers wounded; all deprived of their weapons. Altogether 4 dead and 11 wounded'.

In the course of the war, the 2nd Battalion Arditi Fanti suffered a total of 26 casualties and missing persons.

III Alpine Armed Forces Battalion

It was organised in the Vercelli area in November 1944, already taking the new name of Battaglione Arditi and was initially commanded by Captain Terzoli and later by Major Bergondi. Its structure was:

- 3rd Platoon Command
- 3 Alpine Companies:
    - 9th Alpine Company
    - 10th Alpine Company
    - 11th Alpine Company
- 12th Accompanying Arms Company[35]

It is worth noting that a memo from the Republican Army General Staff reported that a 3rd Battalion of Arditi was already in formation in Cremona in August 1944. Probably, as often noted from the documents of the period, some departments referred to as *'in formation'* were
such only on paper, while in reality these units were not even in an embryonic state.
It is therefore possible that this is the case of the 3rd Arditi Battalion in formation in Cremona, mentioned in this memo
The Battalion had been stationed in Santhià (VC) since its establishment in November 1944. At the beginning of 1945, the main nucleus of the unit was moved to Cigliano Vercellese (VC) and only one Platoon was left in Santhià to guard the town, at the local Carabinieri barracks. From this moment on, the 3rd Battalion of the Alpini Arditi found itself under severe pressure from the intensification of partisan activity. In order to contain the growing ferment of the Resistance, the Battalion was hard at work in a gruelling, almost daily repetition of offensive raids and control actions in the territory where it was stationed. At the end of April 1945, the Battalion was partly in Alba, where it had been sent for rein-

---

[35] This company appears in the organisation chart proposed by Giorgio Pisanò in 'Gli ultimi in Grigioverde', a work cited in the bibliography.

forcement after the attempted partisan attack on the 15th, and partly in Turin. The names of five fallen soldiers of the Battalion are known.

X Special Artillery Group

With the aim of providing artillery support to the R.A.P. units, the 10th Special Artillery Battery was formed, which was already in formation in Brescia on 5 August 1944, under the CO - GU. Already in July, however, a first nucleus of Artillerymen had been concentrated in Novara at the schools in Via Cacciapiatti. On 18 July, 1 officer and 20 artillerymen from the Battery collaborated with a squad of Republican Police Officers and a platoon of 20 militiamen from the Novara Black Brigade on a punitive expedition to Orta (NO), where they arrested members of a cell that was stealing design drawings from an Alfa Romeo plant that had been relocated there to escape the bombing.

The Battery reached Turin, together with the 1st Arditi Battalion of the Anti-Partisan Regiment, on 10 August 1944, and on 18 August the 2nd Section of the Special Battery became part of the 10th MAS.

At the end of August, the 10th Special Battery had one battery stationed at Bard (AO) and one being transferred to Cirié (TO), to be used in counter-guerrilla actions; the Battery's personnel consisted of four officers and 95 non-commissioned officers and troops. In that period the unit had its first two casualties, Artillerymen Giovanni Albè and Angelo Alchiero, who died following an ambush in Aosta on 23 August 1944; they were in all probability in force at the Battery stationed in Bard.

In December 1944, the Battery was transformed into the 10th Special Artillery Group, first into 2 Batteries, then into 4 Batteries:

- Command
- 1st Field Battery
    - I Section on 2 pieces
    - II Section on 2 pieces
- 2nd Field Battery - commander Captain Aldo Lallini
    - I Section on 2 pieces - commander Second Lieutenant Eugenio Petrelli
    - II Section on 2 pieces
- 3rd Field Battery
    - I Section on 2 pieces
    - II Section on 2 pieces
- 4th Heavy Field Battery
    - I Section on 2 pieces
    - II Section on 2 pieces

Commander of the Group was Major Mazzantini. The Batteries, each on 2 Sections of 2 pieces each, were armed with 75/13 pieces; according to Pisanò, the Group was also equipped with 105 (2nd Battery), 100/17 (3rd Battery) and 149 (4th Battery) pieces, but this equipment would seem to be contradicted by Colonel Ruta's report on the liberation of Alba, in which he speaks exclusively of Batteries armed with 75/13 howitzers. Following the liberation of

Alba on 2 November 1944, the 2nd Battery of the 10th Special Artillery Group was stationed in the town, remaining there as a fixed garrison until the end of the conflict.

During the battle of 15 April 1945, the two Sections of the 2nd Battery, which was commanded by Captain Aldo Lallini, were positioned to defend two different strongholds. The 1st Section, under the command of Second Lieutenant Eugenio Petrelli, was sent in support of the 5th Company of the 2nd Battalion Arditi Fanti, at the Minor Seminary in Alba, while the 2nd Section remained in support of the Arditi Fanti Battalion Headquarters at the 'Govone' Barracks, engaging its two pieces in interdiction fire from the early hours of the day. During the fighting, the Battery suffered only a light wound, Artilleryman Vittorio Carpino.

As for the other Republican divisions involved in the clashes of 15 April, we are able to provide the complete transcript of the report of Captain Lallini, commander of the 2nd Battery of the 10th Special Artillery Group[36]:

"<u>X SPECIAL ARTILLERY GROUP</u>
<u>2ND BATTERY</u>

TO COMMAND IIND BTG. ARDITI FANS

<u>HEADQUARTERS</u>

SUBJECT: *Report on the events of 15/4/1945/XXIII°*

In the evening of 14/4, a strong concentration of partisan elements was reported by the Btg. Command in the locality of "Gallo", and in other nearby localities. Given the respectable strength of the reported bands, a strong attack on the Alba garrison was to be assumed. During the night, the IA Section of the battery under the command of S.Lt. Petrelli Eugenio moved into the 5th Comp.'s camps, while the 2nd Section, throughout the night, carried out disturbance and interdiction shots on the reported gathering locations. In the meantime, in conjunction with the cavalry platoon, the guard and neighbouring defence service was reinforced.

At approximately 4 a.m. on 15/4, there was a state of alarm due to the loss of electricity and telephone communication.

At around 6 a.m., preceded by a loud explosion, heavy and light automatic weapons fire began, mainly from the hillside in front of the GOVONI barracks. While the IIA Section from its courtyard opened fire on the surrounding hills. At 6.30 a.m., while the enemy fire was becoming more and more intense and raging, it was noted that outlaw elements, infiltrated in large numbers from Porta Vivaro, had occupied the buildings surrounding the barracks and were opening fire on the courtyards and on the Section, so much so that the pieces, in order not to expose the men uselessly, were withdrawn and placed for close defence, since it was impossible to intervene otherwise, given that every external and internal corner of the barracks was under the precise fire of the outlaws. At about 8.30 a.m., the enemy also intervened with

---

36 In the text, the capitalised spelling of some terms and some spelling errors have been retained, as they are present in the text of the original document. Likewise, an insulting epithet, used against a partisan commander by the officer in his report, has been retained so as not to alter the authenticity of the text and its emphatic style.

mortars and grenade launchers to the extent that the cavalry platoon had to retreat to the main barracks building where the section was deployed, taking one wounded man with them. At 8.30 a.m., Art. Caprino was wounded in the legs by mortar shrapnel.

On our side, in this first phase of the attack, we reacted effectively by repulsing any attempt to approach by the adversaries, who, given the futility of the attacks and the losses inflicted by our fire, formed a deployment of automatic weapons on the periphery of the barracks, initiating a robust siege of fire from a distance (200 - 300 metres).

In the meantime, the fall of the blockade post at Porta Savona was noted, where the partisans themselves settled.

The situation, which was already worrying due to the intense enemy fire, was becoming more and more critical due to the continuous enemy siege, the absolute lack of connections and therefore of news from the other divisions of the garrison of which, given the distance and the strong enemy fire, it was not even possible to notice the possible reaction. Moreover, as the attack was prolonged, the lack of ammunition and food supplies could be felt.

Towards midday, when the situation was particularly delicate for us, through Cav. Amadini, who had fallen prisoner, the partisans demanded our surrender, which was decisively refused, even though we were informed of the almost total destruction of the 8th Comp., the imminent surrender of the 5th and the capture of about 40 prisoners.

From then on, throughout the afternoon, the barracks were kept under constant heavy weapons, mortar and grenade launcher fire, which created unfavourable conditions for defence as every defensive arrangement was taken under a precise barrage.

Around 4 p.m., two "L" wagons of the Btg. finally managed to reach "Govoni" and re-establish a momentary connection. At the same time as the wagons left the barracks, the partisan fire increased in intensity, culminating in the firing of incendiary grenades, which, however, hit unattacked points.

Towards 5 p.m., the enemy fire gradually decreased in intensity while partisan groups could be seen moving away from the area of fire. At 18:00 the fire was reduced to isolated rifle and mortar shots. At 6:30 p.m., a patrol under the command of Lt. Marquez of the 5th Comp. managed to approach our barracks, bringing news of the partisans' retreat from the city. At 7 p.m. a mixed patrol of artillerymen and cavalrymen came out and the situation was normalised as we could see that the adversary had retreated into the hills.

Observations showed that the attackers from the south were part of communist formations under the command of the French bastard 'GIMMI', while the attackers from the north were part of fully equipped, armed and trained G.L. formations.

The behaviour of the men was above all praise, even in the critical moments of the morning and early afternoon, when the enemy's lead was at its strongest, there was never a hesitation but always a cool decision to resist to the bitter end, absolute calm and dosed and intelligent reaction fire. The behaviour of some was even superb.

Casualties: Art. CAPRINO Vittorio, slightly wounded in the legs by mortar shrapnel.

The Commander of the 2nd Battery
Captain Aldo Lallini.

According to the list of the fallen of the Historical Institute of the R.S.I., the known dead and missing of the 10th Special Artillery Group are sixteen, many of whom were picked up and executed at the end of the war; the list is certainly incomplete.

Autonomous Cavalry Department

When the first units of the R.A.P. began to form in the summer of 1944, a number of tanks were recovered in Milan and Turin, which would later be engaged by the newly formed Gruppo Esplorante, quartered at the Scuola d'Applicazione d'Arma in Via Arsenale in Turin. In October, the Army General Staff's Autonomous Cavalry Squadron received orders to create a Cavalry division to be sent to Alba, which was to be liberated from units of the Anti-Partisan Regiment. During the operations for the liberation of Alba, another mounted unit from Cuneo was also employed, whose organic dependence is unknown, and whose commander was Major Bonatelli[37]. However, documents from the General Staff of the E.N.R. show that a XXXX Autonomous Cavalry Group was already being constituted on 5 August 1944 in Bergamo at the General Staff Squadron, reporting to the CO-GU (Contro Guerriglia). The task of setting up the Squadron and commanding it was entrusted to Captain Remo Bussotti, who organised a 60-strong unit. Bussotti's squadron headed for the Piedmontese city, reaching it on 2 November, by which time Alba had been liberated. At the end of the operations, the R.A.P. left some units to garrison, among them the Autonomous Cavalry Squadron, which had just arrived, and from that moment on, the Autonomous Cavalry Department was definitively attached to the R.A.P., with a depot in Turin, and the Exploring Group was thus organised in November 1944:

- Command Squadron commanded by Captain Reno Bozzi;
- Autonomous Cavalry Department commanded by Captain Remo Bussotti[38];
- 1st Tank Company M commanded by Lieutenant Ascanio Caradonna;
- 2nd Tank Company L commanded by Lieutenant Domenico Caruso.

An aliquot of the Autonomous Cavalry Department under the command of Captain Bussotti was stationed in Turin, at the Scuola d'Applicazione d'Arma, to set up the Department Depot[39]. The members of the Department were mainly engaged in armed escort operations to the wagon trains that transported foodstuffs (especially salt!) from Turin to the Cuneo area, as far as Bra. This activity was carried out constantly until the end of the war, without ever having to engage the Cavalrymen in firefights, as the mere presence of the mounted escort was sufficient to deter attackers. The Cavalry Department also operated in support of counter-guerrilla actions conducted by other units of the Anti-Partisan Regiment in the area of operations.

The Platoon detached in Alba carried out its assigned tasks of garrisoning the town of

---

37 Units of the G.N.R. and the Cuneo Black Brigades also took part in the operations to liberate Alba; it cannot be excluded that Major Bonatelli's unit depended on the local command of the National Republican Guard.
38 Giorgio Pisanò, in "Gli ultimi in Grigioverde" (The Last in Grey-green) mentions a certain Lieutenant Cesarini as commander of the Squadron, information that is however denied by the memoirs of Captain Bussotti himself ("Lo Squadrone di Cavalleria dello Stato Maggiore dell'Esercito (e poi del R.A.P.)" in "Acta" number 15, May-July 1991). It cannot be ruled out that Lieutenant Cesarini was the commander of the Cavalry Platoon posted in Alba.
39 Pisanò claims that the Squadron was already at the R.A.P. in August 1944, based at the Scuola d'Applicazione d'Arma in via Arsenale, where it was later joined by the Tank Companies, effectively forming the founding nucleus of the Exploring Group. The same news is taken up by Nava and Corbatti in 'Like Diamond!'. This information, however, is denied by the aforementioned memoirs of the commander of the Autonomous Cavalry Department, Captain Bussotti.

Alba uninterruptedly until 25 April 1945. At the end of the conflict, the Autonomous Department shared the fate of the Anti-Partisan Regiment. Leaving Turin on 28 April, the unit reached the 'free zone' of Strambino Romano with the Turin fascist column, where it surrendered to the Allies on 5 May. The Americans granted the honour of arms to the prisoners, who were temporarily concentrated at the Olivetti factories in Ivrea, before being transferred to the Coltano prison camp. The garrison at Alba was attacked on 26 April and the Republican garrison surrendered after two days of fighting, but the fate of the Knights in the town is unknown. According to the R.S.I. Historical Institute's list of fallen soldiers, the known dead and missing of the Autonomous Cavalry Department number fifteen, although the list is certainly incomplete.

1st Light Tank Company

When the first divisions of the R.A.P. began to form in the summer of 1944, trucks for the Autodrappello and some tanks were recovered in Milan and Turin, which would later be used by the newly formed Gruppo Esplorante. Starting in August, the R.A.P. was moved in stages to Piedmont, where partisan action was most concentrated.

In Turin in November 1944, an L tank company and an M tank company were formed, which were quartered at the Scuola d'Applicazione d'Arma in via Arsenale; the Exploring Group's armoured equipment at this time probably consisted of no more than a dozen L3 tanks and one M tank. As we have seen above, the Gruppo Esplorante was first established as an Autonomous Cavalry Department in Bergamo, with personnel from the Horse Squadron Group of the General Staff of the National Republican Army, later absorbing the Horse Platoon of the C.A.R.S. and then the Tank Companies. On 15 December, two partisans from Turin's G.A.P. took the bait and attempted to assassinate Lieutenant Domenico Caruso, commander of the L Tank Company, while he was walking through the centre of the Piedmontese capital, but the officer's prompt reaction put the two assailants to flight. Lieutenant Caruso was later transferred to another post and was probably replaced by Lieutenant Ernesto Colombiani. The 1st Tank Company M was quickly disbanded, due to lack of resources, and the 2nd Company was renamed the 1st Light Tank Company.

The R.A.P. participated in force in the operations to attack the town of Alba, occupied by the partisans on 2 November 1944 and, as we have seen, after the town's liberation, the R.A.P. left some units in charge, including the Autonomous Cavalry Squadron.

At the end of 1944, the Aufstellungsstab Süd placed at the disposal of the Anti-Partisan Regiment a number of non-functional armoured vehicles, which were lying abandoned at the Caselle depot, vehicles that, at least in part, could have been restored to running condition by the Regiment personnel: 7 L3 light tanks, 1 M13 medium tank, 2 L40 47/32 self-propelled vehicles, 2 75/18 self-propelled vehicles and 1 AB41 armoured car.

During the month of January 1945, a platoon with 4 tanks from the L Tank Company of the Exploring Group was sent to Alba to reinforce the local garrison of the Anti-Partisan Regiment, under the command of Lieutenant Lega Cleto. This platoon also occasionally operated as a reinforcement for the RAU units stationed in Cherasco and later in Bra.

In a circular dated 18 February 1945, the Army General Staff ordered the establishment of the 1st Light Tank Company within the R.A.P., organised on:

- Company Headquarters
- Command Platoon
- 3 L3 Tank Platoons

The Company's staff consisted of 7 officers, 13 non-commissioned officers and 33 tank drivers, with a planned 14 light tanks; from a document dated 23 February 1945, we learn that the unit had, at that date, 1 armoured car (from the photographic documentation, an AB41), 17 L3 tanks, 6 of which were being repaired, 1 L6 (from the photographic documentation, it appears to be a self-propelled L40) and 2 M13 tanks.

In Alba, the tanks of the Platoon detached there were engaged on 16 February to drive away partisans who, in two separate operations in the very early hours of the day, had attempted to assault two checkpoints of the Anti-Partisan Regiment.

On 18 February 1945, the Expeditionary Group was officially formed, with the merger of the 1st Tank Company and the Autonomous Cavalry Department, which from then on was called the Horse Platoon.

On 24 March, a platoon of the Tank Company, reinforced by men from the Horse Platoon, was sent to guard the town of Chieri, at the request of the Army Command Liguria, where a supply depot of the Army was located.

According to a report of 29 March 1945, the Company, stationed in Turin, was staffed by 48 men; there were only 6 light tanks still operational, a Platoon of 3 tanks and their crews was stationed in Alba, while 8 vehicles were under repair.

At the beginning of April, part of the platoon of the L3 Tank Company (probably with only one tank), stationed in Alba, was temporarily transferred to Bra, where the 1st Officer Armed Forces Division was stationed, taking part in some clashes, which ended with the breaking of the encirclement of the town of Alba on 15 April 1945, described in the previous chapter.

As of 5 April 1945, the personnel of Tank Company L was as follows:

- Effective strength: 24 officers, 19 non-commissioned officers, 29 soldiers and 1 auxiliary
- Force present: 16 officers, 5 NCOs, 27 soldiers and 1 auxiliary

On the same day, the light tank section stationed in Alba took part in a round-up between Roddi and Verduno. The clashes with the partisans became more and more intense, so much so that on 6 April, the R.A.P. Tank Company lost two armoured cars[40] and the L40 self-propelled vehicle during bloody clashes in Cisterna d'Asti.

The report written by the commander of the Alba Tank Section on the events of 15 April 1945 is interesting, allowing us to learn more details about the actions of the armoured men during the clashes:

"Having begun the partisan attack at 6.30 a.m. on 15.4.45, at 8.30 a.m. on the orders of the major commander I went out with two wagons from the S. Secondo depot to see and report on the situation in the town and in particular on the situation of the roadblocks.

I arrived at Porta Torino and found no abnormalities; I then continued to the checkpoint

---

[40] The documents quoted above only attest to the presence of an AB41 with the Armoured Company of the R.A.P., but photographs taken at the end of the clash show a Lancia Lince in the hands of the partisans in Cisterna; this armoured reconnaissance car was probably also employed by the Armoured Company of the R.A.P. and this would be the second armoured car mentioned among the losses on 6 April 1945 (see Nava, Corbatti, 'Like the Diamond!').

for Porta Vivaro where there was also nothing abnormal. I reached Piazza Savona and here I noticed a large number of partisans and was greeted by a large number of automatic and individual weapons. Given where the partisans were coming from, I judged it appropriate to push on to Via Mazzini at Stipel. Here I stopped, having noticed an individual bending over the rubble blocking the road. Not judging it opportune to continue beyond the rubble, I repeated the route I had already taken, always followed by enemy fire.

I then noticed that the tank of S. Lt. Vari Ardenio's tank was not following me. I walked the route a few more times and finding no trace of the said tank, I went back to the depot and reported the situation to the major commander. After about an hour I went out again to report the situation at Porta Torino. Along the way I was always accompanied by partisan automatic weapons fire and at the entrance to the City Cathedral I noticed a corpse. I went again to Piazza Savona, where the situation was still the same. Later I went out a third time to support the platoon of Lt. Marquez's platoon, which was coming out of the S. Secondo encampment. Reaching Piazza della Repubblica, I preceded him into Piazza Savona. Here I was not greeted by any discharges, while I noticed that four individuals were closing in on a block of flats in the square. Judging that they were Lt. Marquez, I did not fire and returned to report.

I went out again to support the retreat of the men of the Porta Cherasca blockade post, who with my protection and under the fire of an adversary heavy weapon managed to fall back to the S. Secondo provision. I went out again with Capt. Rossi on board and with a second wagon to find out the situation of the Porta Savona blockade post and the Govone Barracks. When I reached Piazza Savona, I was greeted by the usual enemy fire. I judged it opportune to fall back to the barracks as it was impossible to get an idea of the situation at the Porta Savona checkpoint. I went out again to carry an order from the major commander to the Govone Barracks. There I stayed for about half an hour and returned to the barracks with the news of that detachment. I went out again to support a squad that was going to the 8th Company detachment located in the Convitto Civico. I then went to the Porta Vivaro checkpoint near the Civil Hospital.

By order of the major commander I went out twice more, taking myself as far as the broken bridge over the Tanaro, trying to signal my presence to elements of the reinforcement column, who had arrived on the other side of the Tanaro. The Tank Section suffered the following losses in men during the partisan attack: S. Lt. Vari Ardenio, Capt. Maj. Cacciotti Gabriele. With regard to material, the partisans removed the two Breda 38 machine guns from the immobilised tank, a machine gun and two pistols, the crew's individual armament.

The bodies of the tank were recovered. During this action, 1,080 rounds were fired from my tank. As for the tank of s. lieutenant Vari, it is not possible to specify the number of shots fired as the partisans removed all the magazines.

In memory of S. Lt. Vari and Capt. Maj. Cacciotti were awarded the silver medal in the field for their heroic conduct in combat'.

At the end of the clashes, the Tank Platoon, with a staff reduced to only three L3 tanks, was left in Alba to reinforce the 2nd Battalion Arditi, where it remained until the end of the war, carrying out a few reinforcement raids on the units of the I R.A.U. stationed in Cherasco and Bra.

The garrison in Alba was again attacked on 26 April and the Republican garrison surrendered after two days of fighting. The fate of the tank drivers in the town is unknown, but certainly the 3 light tanks of the R.A.P. were confiscated by the partisans of the 'Langhe' Division, as witnessed by some photographs. The bulk of the R.A.P.'s armoured division, stationed in Turin, followed the fate of the Republican column that surrendered to the Americans in the free zone of Ivrea on 5 May.

According to the casualty list of the R.S.I. Historical Institute, the only known casualties of the R.A.P.'s armoured division are the two tank men who fell in Alba on 15 April.

▲ Canadian soldiers from the Canuck mission in Castino with two cars.

▲ A group of partisans drive towards Alba during the 25 April uprising in a civilian car (WEB source).

▲ One of the L3 of the R.A.P. Light Tank Company stationed in Alba, captured by partisans at the end of the war. Under the handmade inscription 'II DIV. LANGHE" it is still possible to see the republican tricolour, which was placed on almost all R.A.P. armoured vehicles; towing a cannon, probably German.

▼ Captain Robert 'Buck' MacDonald, commander of the Canuck mission, in a modified car during the operations that led to the liberation of Alba (WEB source).

▲ Partisans in Alba aboard an abandoned light wagon of the Anti-Partisan Regiment (Crippa).

▼ The war is over: on the square in Alba, the three light tanks of the R.A.P. Tank Company section stationed in the Piedmontese city are now in the hands of the insurgents.

▲ Partisan leaders enter liberated Alba (Manes).

▼ Military, civil and religious authorities greeted the crowd from the balcony of the town hall on the evening of 26 or the morning of 27 April 1945: among them was Bishop Grassi, who had great influence in the military affairs of the Piedmontese city during the two years of civil war (Studio Agnelli Alba).

▲ Partisans of the 21st Matteotti Brigade 'Ambrogio Brothers' in a posed photo immediately after the liberation of Alba (WEB source).

▼ Partisans of the 'Belbo' Brigade on the heights around Alba ('Alba for Freedom').

▲ Partisans of the 'Langhe' Division photographed in the centre of Alba at the Liberation (Mattia Barbero collection).

▼ A Dovunque 41 truck, loaded with partisans: the use of the 'personalised' plate with the words 'DIVISIONE LANGHE' is remarkable (Mattia Barbero collection).

▲ After liberating Alba, elements of the Langhe partisan formations participated in the parades that celebrated the 'Liberation' in Turin (source: WEB).

▼ After the clashes that led to the city's liberation, on 30 April 1945 the partisans arrested Major Gagliardo Gagliardi, commander of the 2nd Battalion of Arditi Fanti (indicated by number 1), and Captain Amleto Rossi (indicated by number 2), commander of the 5th Company of the same Battalion, in Alba (Pisanò).

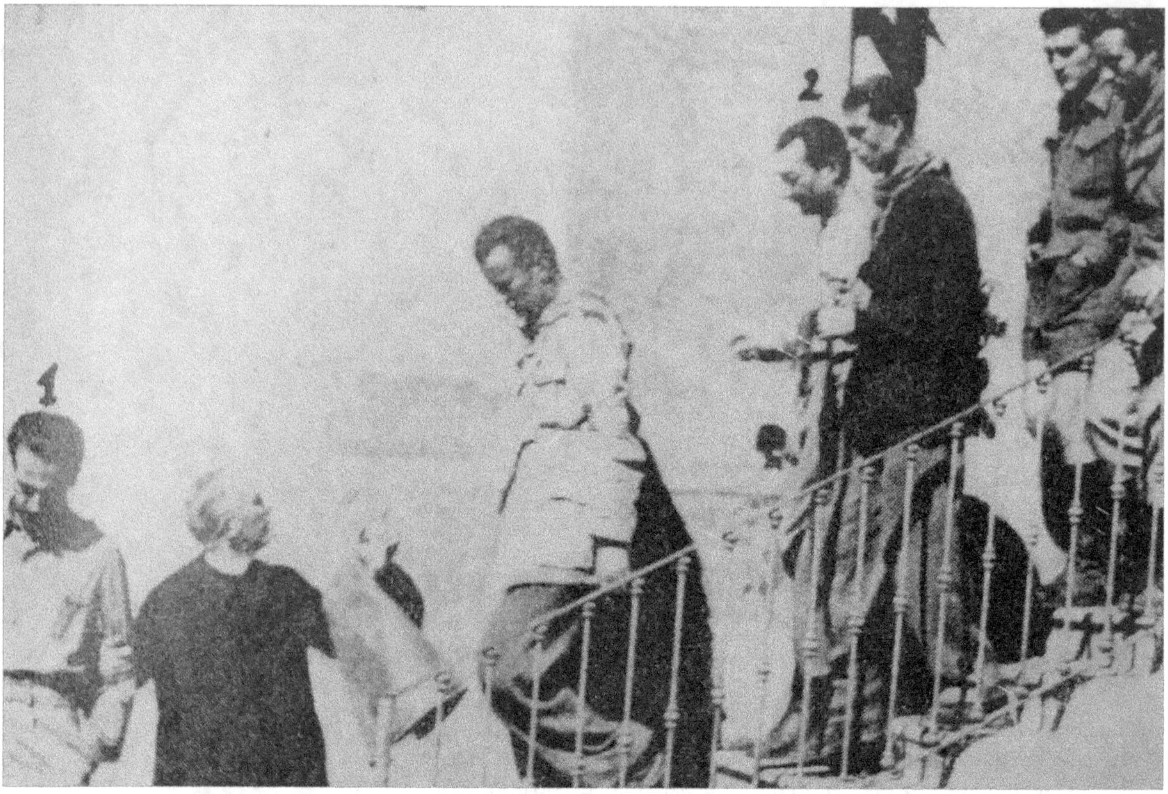

▲ Major Gagliardo Gagliardi (indicated by number 1) and Captain Amleto Rossi (indicated by number 2) at the end of the trial that sentenced them to death (Pisanò).

▼ The two officers of the Anti-Partisan Grouping, Major Gagliardi (indicated with number 1) and Captain Rossi (indicated with number 2), are taken to the cemetery in Alba, where they will be shot (Pisanò).

▲ In 2000, the film 'Il partigiano Jonny' (The Partisan Jonny) was made, based on Beppe Fenoglio's autobiographical novel of the same name, as most of the events, although fictionalised, were actually experienced by the author in the first person. In the photograph, an image from the set of the film which, in an overall view of the partisans arriving in Piazza Duomo in Alba in October 1944, renders the atmosphere experienced in the Piedmontese city at that time (source: WEB).

BIBLIOGRAPHY

Books

- AA.VV, "Le missioni alleate e le formazioni dei partigiani autonomi nella Resistenza piemontese: atti del Convegno internazionale: Torino, 21-22 ottobre 1978", Edizioni L'Arciere.
- AA.VV., "Alba per la Libertà, Regione Piemonte, 1984.
- AA.VV., "Soldati e Battaglie della Seconda Guerra Mondiale", Hobby & Work Italiana Editrice, 1998.
- Ambrosio Piero, "I notiziari della G.N.R. della Provincia di Vercelli all'attenzione del Duce", Istituto per la storia della Resistenza e della società contemporanea nel Biellese, nel Vercellese e in Valsesia, Varallo Sesia (VC), 2012.
- Amedeo Renzo, "Alba Libera", Centro Studi Partigiani autonomi, Torino, 1980.
- Amedeo Renzo, "Storia partigiana della Divisione Autonoma XV Alessandria", Autonomi Editorie, 1983
- Arena Nino, "R.S.I. – Forze Armate della Repubblica Sociale – La guerra in Italia – 1943 – 1944 – 1945", Ermanno Albertelli Editore.
- Bocca Giorgio, "Partigiani della montagna. Vita delle divisioni "Giustizia e Libertà" del Cuneese", Feltrinelli.
- Christin Francesco, "Con gli alamari nella RSI. Storia del 1° Battaglione Granatieri di Sardegna 1943/45", Settimo Sigillo, 1995.
- Ciavattone Federico, "Gli Specialisti – I Reparti Arditi ufficiali e la Squadra X nella lotta antipartigiana – 1944- '45", Mattioli 1885, Fidenza (PR), 2014.
- Conti Arturo, "Albo caduti e dispersi della Repubblica Sociale Italiana", FONDAZIONE DELLA R.S.I. - ISTITUTO STORICO ONLUS.
- Corbatti Sergio, Nava Marco, "Come il diamante", Laran Editions
- Corbatti Sergio e Nava Marco, "Sentire - Pensare - Volere Storia della Legione SS italiana", Ritter.
- Crippa Paolo, "I Reparti Corazzati della Repubblica Sociale Italiana 1943 -1945", Marvia Edizioni, Voghera (PV), 2005.
- Crippa Paolo, "Italia 43 -45 – I blindati di circostanza della Guerra Civile", Mattioli 1885, Fidenza (PR), 2014.
- Crippa Paolo, "I mezzi corazzati italiani della Guerra Civile 43- 45", Mattioli 1885, Fidenza (PR), 2015.
- Cucut Carlo e Crippa Paolo, "I reparti controguerriglia della R.S.I. C.A.R.S. - Cacciatori degli Appennini - R.A.P"., Marvia Edizioni, Voghera (PV), 2020.
- Crippa Paolo, "Storia dei Reparti Corazzati della Repubblica Sociale Italiana 1943 -1945", Marvia Edizioni, Voghera (PV), 2022.
- Cucut Carlo, "Le Forze Armate della R.S.I. 1943 – 1945 – Forze di terra", G.M.T.
- Cucut Carlo, Bobbio Roberto, "Attilio Viziano – Ricordi di un corrispondente di guerra", Marvia Edizioni.

- Fenoglio Beppe, I ventitré giorni della città di Alba, 2022 Einaudi
- Gamberini Maurizio e Maculan Riccardo, "Battaglione Fulmine. X Flottiglia MAS. 1944-1945. Documenti ed immagini", Editrice Lo Scarabeo, 1994.
- Gamberini Maurizio, Maculan Riccardo, "Battaglione Fulmine – Xª Flottiglia MAS 1944 – 1945", Edizioni Menin, Schio (VI), 2009.
- Gentile Carlo, "I servizi segreti tedeschi in Italia, 1943-1945" tratto da Paolo Ferrari e Massignani Alessandro, "Conoscere il nemico. Apparati di intelligence e modelli culturali nella storia contemporanea", Franco Angeli.
- Grandi Marco, "La relazione sull'attività del Gruppo Divisioni Autonome "Mauri" (Settembre 1943-Aprile 1945)", Editrice Ipotesi.
- Griner Massimiliano, "La "Pupilla" del Duce. La Legione autonoma mobile Ettore Muti", Bollati Boringhieri.
- Iebole Ferruccio, "Partigiani, martiri liguri, piemontesi e Cacciatori degli Appennini", Edizione AEC Resistenza – Album della Guerra di Liberazione", Rizzoli, Milano, 1995.
- Martini Mauri Enrico, "Partigiani penne nere. Boves, Val Maudagna, Val Casotto, le Langhe", Edizioni il Capricorno.
- Martini Mauri Enrico, "Con la libertà e per la libertà", Società Editrice Torinese, 1947.
- Masera Diana, "Langa partigiana "43-"45", Araba Fenice.
- Nava Marco, "La 34. Infanterie Division sul fronte italiano 1944-1945", edito in proprio
- Perona Gianni, "Formazioni autonome nella Resistenza. Documenti", Istituto Nazionale per la storia del movimento di liberazione in Italia.
- Pisanò Giorgio, "Gli ultimi in grigioverde", Edizioni F.P.E.
- Pisanò Giorgio, "Storia della Guerra Civile in Italia", Edizioni F.P.E.
- Rocco Giuseppe, "Con l'Onore per l'Onore – L'organizzazione militare della R.S.I. sul finire della Seconda Guerra Mondiale", Greco & Greco Editori.
- Rossi Andrea, "Arditi di ritorno. Le alterne fortune dell'arditismo nella Repubblica Sociale Italiana", in "Eunomia Rivista semestrale di Storia e Politica Internazionali", numero 2, 2015, Università del Salento.
- S.A., "Alba per la libertà", Regione Piemonte, 1984.
- Sandri Leonardo, "la 356^ Infanterie Division sul fronte italiano 1943-1945", edito in proprio, 2020.
- Sandri Leonardo, "Raggruppamento 'Cacciatori degli Appennini'. Una documentazione", edito in proprio, 2020.
- Sparacino Franco, "Distintivi e medaglie della R.S.I." Editrice Militare Italiana.
- Stefani Maurizio, "Struttura e organizzazione del Primo Gruppo Divisioni Alpine", Edizioni Autonomi.
- Toscani Gianni, "Con i partigiani in Valbormida, Valle Uzzone, Valle Belbo – Langhe. Interviste – documenti – fotografie", Magema Edizioni, 2007.

Magazines

- Barbano Filippo, "I fatti militari di Alba in alcuni documenti partigiani e repubblicani (10 ottobre 1944 – 15 aprile 1945)" in "Il movimento di liberazione in Italia" numero 4, a cura dell'I.N.S.M.L.I., senza editore, 1950.
- Conti Arturo, "Albo caduti e dispersi della Repubblica Sociale Italiana", Fondazione della R.S.I. – Istituto Storico, Terranuova Bracciolini (AR), 2018.
- De Luca Giampaolo, "Partigiani delle Langhe. Cultura di banda e rapporti tra formazioni nella VI zona operativa piemontese", Università degli Studi di Pisa, A.A. 2012-13.
- Favrin Roberta, "Lotta partigiana e società contadina: L"VIII^ Divisione Garibaldi "Asti"", Istituto per la storia della Resistenza e della società contemporanea in Provincia di Asti.
- Monsignor Grassi Luigi, "Ricordi personali", in "La tortura di Alba e dell'Albese", Alba, 1946.
- Renzo Amedeo, "Diario Mauri. Marzo 1945", in "Autonomi", Torino, 1980.
- Renzo Amedero, "Diario Mauri. Dicembre 1944", in "Autonomi", Torino, 1979.
- Rivero Michele, "Il tribunale delle grandi unità CARS – COGU (Sull'amministrazione della giustizia militare nella Repubblica di Salò)" in "Il Movimento di Liberazione in Italia", a cura dell'I.N.S.M.L.I., numero 25, senza editore, 1953.
- Ruzzi Marco, "Dalla RSI alle formazioni partigiane. Analisi di un percorso", I.S.R.A.T. Asti.
- Ruzzi Marco, "Presenza ed attività delle Forze della RSI in provincia di Asti", I.S.R.A.T., Asti.
- Ruzzi Marco, "La X Divisione Giustizia e Libertà", I.S.R.A.T. Asti.
- Scalpelli Adolfo, "La formazione delle forze armate di Salò attraverso i documenti dello Stato Maggiore della R.S.I." in "Il movimento di liberazione in Italia" numeri 72 e 73, a cura dell'I.N.S.M.L.I., senza editore, 1963.
- "Acta", numeri vari, Fondazione della R.S.I. - Istituto Storico, Terranuova Bracciolini (AR).
- "Uniformi ed armi", numeri vari, Ermanno Albertelli Editore, Parma.
- Grassi Luigi Maria (Vescovo di Alba), "La tortura di Alba e dell'Albese (Settembre 1943 – Aprile 1945) – Ricordi personali".

TITOLI GIÀ PUBBLICATI - TITLES ALREADY PUBLISHING

BOOKS TO COLLECT

www.ingramcontent.com/pod-product-compliance
Lightning Source LLC
LaVergne TN
LVHW081538070526
838199LV00056B/3706